INTERNATIONAL LENDING:
Country Risk Analysis

Emilio Mayer

Reston Financial Services
Division of Reston Publishing Company, Inc.
Reston, Virginia

Library of Congress Cataloging in Publication Data
Mayer, Emilio.
    International lending: country risk analysis.
    Includes index.
    1. Loans, Foreign—Evaluation. I. Title.
HG3891.5.M39   1985   336.3'435   84-16048
ISBN 0-8359-3182-X

Interior design and production by Alice Cave

© 1985 by Reston Publishing Company, Inc.
A *Prentice Hall Company*
Reston, Virginia 22090

10   9   8   7   6   5   4   3   2   1

Printed in the United States of America

Contents

List of Tables

Preface

In view of the enormous amounts of money involved in international lending, one would expect to find a dozen textbooks and a wide range of reference material on international creditworthiness evaluation systems and procedures. But that is not the case. Numerous articles have been published during the last few years on various aspects of evaluation procedures, but overall, comprehensive textbooks are still missing.

The purpose of this book is to fill some of the vacuum. The overall problem will be discussed from a practical point of view. An attempt will be made to summarize traditional evaluation systems used by commercial banks in the United States and abroad. Some new evaluation methods will be explored.

The book does not purport to offer permanent solutions. It is intended to stimulate imaginative thinking among international analysts. The field is wide and, in my opinion, only at an initial stage of exploration.

This kind of book is never complete. Changing techniques, new ideas and availability of additional data would require continuous amendments and updating.

I am deeply indebted to those who assisted me by supplying information, making suggestions, and offering their criticism. I am especially grateful to Leonard W. Ascher for his patience in reading various drafts and for his invaluable overall advice, and to Albert M. Wojnilower and William W. Sihler for their constructive suggestions. I wish to express my special appreciation to my friends in the international banking community: without their help this book could not have been completed.

E. M.

I

Introduction and Overview

chapter 1

Purpose of Study

International payment difficulties came to public attention on August 20, 1982 when Mexico's finance minister announced to a meeting of foreign creditors that his country could not repay its foreign debts on time. More than two dozen countries followed Mexico's example in the next 18 months.

At the beginning some observers spoke of liquidity crises, but as time went by, it became apparent that the problem was much more serious, that some countries were heavily in debt, probably beyond their immediate repayment capability.

The fact that almost all international banks were competing to lend money to Argentina, Brazil, Chile, Mexico, Venezuela, and so on, indicates that something was fundamentally wrong with the decisionmaking procedures of the lending banks.

One may hypothesize that country risk analysis procedures were basically unsatisfactory, or that management did not have much faith in the work of the analysts and therefore tended to disregard their evaluations, or that management was carried away in the heat of competition, or, more probably, that all these factors contributed to the overspending and overlending which brought about the payment difficulties.

EXTERNAL DEBT ACCUMULATION

The debt accumulation did not happen overnight and did not go unnoticed.

David O. Beim remarked in August 1977 that the "desire to keep the rate of (economic) growth going, while also paying the higher oil prices, has caused the debts of the developing countries to compound at the annual rate of about 25 percent in the last three years, 1974 through 1976. This rate of growth of debt is far in excess of any possible growth in the abilities of countries to carry the debt, and the disproportion cannot continue for much longer."[1]

A few years later in June 1981, Henry C. Wallich repeated the warning "these illustrative calculations (external debt to GNP) serve no other purpose than to demonstrate that today we are in a transitional phase that in the long run is not sustainable. In the short run it is made to appear sustainable, in some degree, by inflation, which causes a country to amortize its debt via interest rates. Fundamentally a good number of countries are borrowing amounts that cannot be continued far into the future without leading to debt burdens that appear unsustainable from historical experience."[2]

The usual procedure to determine the level of indebtedness of a group of countries is to calculate average ratios; but that gives only a partial picture. To obtain a better indication of a deteriorating or improving risk situation, one should identify the countries with the worst ratios, because countries in good financial shape are not going to pay the debts of those unable to pay.

This procedure was followed to compile Table 17 (see Chapter 12) which shows the two worst ratios of Total Interest Due on External Debt as Percentage of Gross External Revenues in a group of 34 countries for the last 20 years. Gross External Revenues (GER) include all foreign exchange earned plus unrequited transfers received. The table shows that the two worst ratios increased more than three times from 6.7 and 9.2 percent in 1960, to 22.8 and 31.7 percent for Bolivia and Brazil respectively in 1980. By 1980, almost four months of Brazil's foreign exchange earnings were preempted for the payment of interest due on foreign debt.

It is obvious that the accumulation of external debt could not continue much longer.

---

[1]David O. Beim. "Financing and Risk in Developing Countries." In *Proceeding of a Symposium on Developing Countries' Debt*. Sponsored by the Export-Import Bank of the United States, August 1977; Chapter 7, Panel Discussion: Private Bank Lending and the Debt Situation of the Developing Countries, p. 62.
[2]Henry C. Wallich. "LDC Debt—To Worry or Not to Worry," Remarks at Bankers' Association for Foreign Trade Convention, Boca Raton, Florida, June 1981.

EVENTS THAT PRECIPITATED PAYMENT DIFFICULTIES

Payment difficulties were precipitated by two concomitant unfavorable developments, both beyond control of debtor countries: first, a sudden increase of international interest rates in real terms, and, second, a global economic slowdown which caused a sharp decline in commodity demand and prices.

A comparison of London Interbank Offer Rate (LIBOR), on one year Eurodollar deposits, with United States Consumer Prices Index (CPI) increases, tells the first part of the story:

Yearly rate for	1978	1979	1980	1981	1982
LIBOR rate	9.3	11.7	13.4	16.0	13.5
USA CPI increase	7.6	11.3	13.5	10.4	6.2
Estimated real rate of return	1.7	0.4	−0.1	5.6	7.3

Source: *International Financial Statistics* (IFS), December 1983.

Since a very substantial share of the international indebtedness was on a short–term basis, due within two or three years, and rollovers were made at LIBOR rates plus a spread, the results of the increase of real interest rates were devastating. For three years, from 1978 to 1980, real interest rates were negligible so that borrowers felt that interest payments were in effect amortizing external debts; but in 1981, the situation changed suddenly and interest payments became a real burden.

The second change was just as dramatic, as shown by the following figures:

	1978	1979	1980	1981	1982
Global export of goods increase, in U.S. dollar terms	15.2	27.7	22.5	−1.4	−7.6
U.S. CPI increase	7.6	11.3	13.5	10.4	6.2
Estimated global exports increase in real terms	7.6	16.4	9.0	−11.8	−13.8

Source: *International Financial Statistics* (IFS), December 1983.

Although the CPI gives only an approximate indication of changes in the dollar's purchasing power, and LIBOR does not represent exactly actual interest rates paid by borrowers, the two variables give a close enough picture of what was going on. Exports of goods, on the other hand, are the bread and butter of most developing countries' foreign exchange earnings, so that the comparison of the two sets of figures explains the euphoria of 1979/1980 and the rude shock of 1981/1982. In the first two years, negligible interest rates in real terms, probably in the one half to one and one half percent range (considering the spread over LIBOR), were compared with export increases of 16 and 9 percent; in the following two years export decreases of 12 to 13 percent were faced with 6 to 7 percent debit interest rates.

ANALYST/MANAGEMENT COMMUNICATIONS

As to why banks continued to expand international lending while the external debts of many borrowers were reaching dangerous levels, and after several observers expressed their concern about the deteriorating situation, one may guess that poor analyst/management communications were probably the main contributory factor.

Therefore, this book is addressed to both analysts and management with the intent of giving a practical update of the state of the art of country risk evaluation procedures, and giving a better understanding of the problems involved in the evaluation process. Moreover, some suggestions will be made about the better use of new data which are becoming available and new analytical methods which should be explored.

The decisionmaking executive has to rely on the evaluations prepared by analysts. He should know how the assessments are made. He should have the basic knowledge which will allow him to make decisions on the basis of reports submitted by analysts. The executive should also be aware of the limitations and the uncertainty of international creditworthiness assessments.

The selection of the level of discussion of international creditworthiness problems, and the decision on what to include or exclude and how far to go with the discussion of conceptual approaches or practical methodology, involve difficulties not found in the case of texts for well-established fields. Some readers may not be happy with the selections or decisions made.

PURPOSE

The purpose of this book is to discuss international creditworthiness evaluation systems, mainly from the viewpoint of private lenders whose only concern is the timely payment of interest and principal of the loans made.

Procedures at present in use for the international creditworthiness analysis will be examined as to their usefulness and limitations in Chapters 3 to 6. Some analytical techniques and methods which are not now commonly used will be discussed in subsequent chapters.

chapter 2

Dissimilarities Between Domestic and International Lending

International lending is exposed to some risks which are not incurred in domestic lending. Such risks are commonly known as:

— country risk
— transfer risk
— economic risk
— political risk and
— sovereign risk.

There is a regrettable lack of uniformity in the use of these terms. Some analysts equate country risk with sovereign risk; others transfer risk with country risk, and so on. To avoid misunderstanding, the meanings attributed to such terms in this book are briefly discussed below.

COUNTRY RISK

Country risk is the additional risk incurred when lending to a foreign country, or to a borrower residing in a foreign country, on top of the usual commercial risk incurred in domestic lending.

Country risk is an overall concept which includes the risks listed above. The meaning of country risk may be best explained by an example.

A bank lends money to a foreign corporation doing business in a foreign country. The foreign corporation will probably do most of its business in local currency. At any rate, it will be subject to the laws and regulations in force in the country where it is doing business.

A situation may arise in which the foreign corporation has the local currency needed to pay all of its obligations, but

— may be unable to obtain the foreign exchange needed to pay foreign creditors, or it

— may have the needed foreign exchange but be prevented from transferring it abroad by local laws or regulations.

The nonpayment is not due to the inability of the foreign corporation to pay its obligations, but to the inability to convert domestic currency into foreign exchange and to transfer it abroad.

A similar situation may arise if the loan is made to, or guaranteed by, a government. Although a government could levy taxes or print money to pay its domestic obligations, it cannot levy taxes abroad or print foreign money to pay external debts. The nonpayment is due to its inability to convert domestic currency into foreign exchange. Of course, there is also the possibility that a government may refuse to pay its obligations (see "Political Risk").

The terms *country risk* and *international creditworthiness* are not mirror images. Country risk covers both the risk incurred when making equity investments in a country and the risk incurred when granting loans to the government or a resident of a country.

Neither do the terms *international creditworthiness* and *external repayment capability* have the same meaning. The external repayment capability is based on the present and potential ability of a country to generate the foreign exchange needed to pay its external debts. Repayment capability is the foundation on which international creditworthiness rests, but there are other factors to be considered in evaluating creditworthiness. For instance, the debtor country may have the repayment capability but uses the foreign exchange for purposes other than paying external debts. However, if there is no external repayment capability, there is no creditworthiness.

TRANSFER RISK

The risk that a borrower who has domestic currency to pay his debts may be prevented from paying by the inability to obtain, or to transfer, the foreign exchange needed to pay external obligations is called transfer risk.

Transfer restrictions in force in countries that are members of the International Monetary Fund (IMF) are summarized in the *Annual Report—Exchange Arrangements and Restrictions* published by the IMF (see Chapter 12, under "Exchange Restrictions").

Whether there is a transfer risk involved when a loan is made in local currency depends on the circumstances. For instance, if a bank has a branch with local deposits in a country, then there would be no transfer risk. The loan would be part of local lending operations; it would be a domestic loan in the host country. On the other hand, if the lender converted foreign currency in order to create the local currency to be lent, then the lender would run not only the risk that the funds may not be transferable when the loan becomes due, but also the risk that the local currency may have been devalued while the loan was outstanding.

✓ Transfer problems may be caused by economic conditions, or by political actions of a government, or both.

The following classification should help to determine the extent of transfer risk involved in various kinds of international lending:

A. Credits extended to private enterprises without government guaranties of any kind.

B. Credits to banks.

C. Credits to private enterprises with the guarantee of a foreign government for the transfer of funds abroad.

D. Credits to private enterprises with unconditional guarantee of repayment by a foreign government.

E. Direct credits to a foreign government.

For category A, the lender relies on foreign exchange transfer regulations in force when the loan is made. If the external accounts of the debtor's country deteriorate, exchange and transfer regulations may be changed, so that the transfer abroad of the funds for the payment of interest due and/or the repayment of principal due, may be delayed or become impossible.

Banks should be placed in a separate category. Although their obligations may not have an explicit government foreign exchange transfer guarantee, the importance of their credit standing in the international financial community is such that banks would normally have a priority in the allocation of foreign exchange.

ECONOMIC RISK

Economic risk is caused by indigenous or exogenous economic developments, such as poor crops, economic policies that cause high domestic demand, decline in demand and prices of a country's exports, all of which adversely affect the balance of payments of a country.

Defaults due to revolutionary changes in government have been infrequent during the last few decades; outright refusals to pay external debts happened only in Cuba, Ghana, and South East Asia when Soviet–oriented regimes took over. On the other hand, payment difficulties due to economic causes happen with disconcerting regularity.

Insufficient foreign exchange generating capability is by far the most common cause of international payments difficulties. The collectability of external obligations depends on the capability of a debtor country—or of a foreign country of which the debtor is a resident—to generate the foreign exchange needed to pay external obligations. If foreign exchange cannot be generated in sufficient quantity, external obligations cannot be paid.

POLITICAL RISK

Political risks are caused by noneconomic factors that affect the availability of foreign exchange or the willingness of the authorities to meet promptly their external obligations or to make available to a country's residents the foreign exchange needed to pay their external obligations.

Adverse social and political developments include war, revolution, riots, or disorders that may lead to a takeover of power by a different government. The new government may not recognize previous external obligations, or may enact expropriation laws, or confiscatory taxation, or other laws or regulations that would prevent the borrower from paying his external obligations.

Post-war experience shows that even when revolutionary changes take place, the new government in most instances recognizes old external obligations. The decision is based on economic considerations. The new government weighs the advantage of being able to rely on future international borrowing on the basis of its good payment record against the short-term advantage of not paying existing debts.

The importance of violent political events as a cause of credit losses has probably been overestimated in country risk evaluations.

SOVEREIGN RISK

Strictly speaking, sovereign risk means the risk involved when doing business with a sovereign government or its instrumentalities.

In international financial circles however the term sovereign risk is used in a broader sense, to indicate the risk of subjecting a transaction to an additional jurisdiction: the borrower's government.

What happens in international lending is that the lender and the borrower are residents of two different, independent countries, which have different—

sometimes contradictory—sets of laws and regulations, that affect both lender and borrower.

What worries creditors more than the many complicated legal problems caused by existing legislation is the risk of future unfavorable action by a borrower's government, e.g., new more stringent limitations or prohibition to transfer funds abroad, moratoria, new crippling taxes, or other laws or regulations that adversely affect external creditors.

Ironically, the creditor may also be adversely affected by legislation originating in his own country due to the freezing of funds, export prohibitions, and so on.

In general, external creditors are less exposed to unfavorable new foreign legislation than foreign investors.

COMMERCIAL RISK

A commercial risk is involved when the loan is not granted directly to a foreign government, or when a foreign government does not fully guarantee a loan.

Commercial risk materializes when a nonofficial borrower is in financial difficulties and cannot pay his obligations, whether domestic or foreign.

The underlying concepts for the evaluation of commercial risks abroad are similar to those applying to domestic risks, but the availability and nature of information on prospective borrowers are different in each country. Thus, it is not feasible to use a standard evaluation system.

Inflation and drastic currency devaluations, economic stagnation, or recession affect each borrower in different ways: loans will have to be assessed on a case by case basis.

New transfer restrictions and severe currency devaluations are the most dangerous eventualities for private borrowers (see Chapter 12, PRIVATE BORROWERS).

chapter 3

Conceptual and Practical Problems

Dragoslav Avramovic described the overall limitations and uncertainties of international creditworthiness evaluation procedures as follows: "The appraisal of creditworthiness of anybody—be it an individual, a business firm, or a country—is a mixture of facts and judgments. Even if we had the theory of debt servicing capacity and could satisfactorily explain the likely behavior of major variables and their time-path, we would still be facing the uncertainties arising from current economic and financial policies which the decision makers in the borrowing countries may choose to adopt, be it at their own initiative or in response to all sorts of pressures."[1]

Avramovic's appraisal of the uncertainty of creditworthiness evaluations is still valid today. There has been no dramatic breakthrough during the last twenty years although considerable time and money have been spent in efforts to find better evaluation systems, mostly by building various models which became progressively more complicated by including more variables. The results have been disappointing.

While efforts to improve international creditworthiness evaluation procedures should not be abandoned, it would seem that the approach should be changed. Instead of searching for overall solutions, one should recognize that

---

[1]Dragoslav Avramovic, et al. *Economic Growth and External Debt*. Published for the World Bank by The Johns Hopkins University Press, Baltimore, Maryland, 1964; Chapter 1 Introduction, under 4. Limitations, pp. 7–8.

the evaluation is a mixture of facts and judgments, and, therefore, that the evaluation process should be subdivided into sections to be examined separately.

As a start, one should consider separately the two concepts of *creditworthiness* and *credit risk*. Most observers consider the concepts as being mirror images: good creditworthiness means small risk and vice versa. That of course is correct. But one should go one step further. Creditworthiness is based on present repayment capability, while credit risk arises from future events, most of them not predictable with any degree of accuracy. Following this line of reasoning, the evaluation problem should be considered from the viewpoint of:

— a country's external repayment capability and the vulnerability of external revenues to exogenous factors,
— risks arising from social and political factors.

The distinction is important because social and political risks are of secondary importance if a country does not have the structural ability to pay its external debts. The evaluation of the external repayment capability is a good starting point because the factors affecting it are quantifiable and, thus, offer a factual basis for the evaluation.

TECHNICAL PROBLEMS

The layman may be inclined to believe that the quantification of factual variables should be a simple matter. In practice however that is not the case.

Hundreds of economic data, most of them relevant in one way or another for a creditworthiness evaluation, are available, but it is not feasible to work all of them into any system or model, so that a selection has to be made about what should be included or left out.

Next, one has to select a base period for the evaluation. Should one, for instance, accept last year's increase of exports as indicative of future trends, or should one consider two, three, or five-year periods as being more reliable?

Then there is the problem of assigning a weight to each variable. Is an increase of export earnings, for instance, more significant for a creditworthiness evaluation than the relative size of a current account deficit?

It is obvious that evaluations will differ if some variables are selected instead of others, or if more or less weight is given to certain variables, or if one period is taken as basis instead of another.

These problems are discussed in Chapter 11, SELECTION OF EVALUATION PROCEDURE, where several suggestions are made with the intent of minimizing judgmental factors.

In the last analysis, however, the selection of variables to be used remains a judgmental matter, but that cannot be avoided.

NO DEFINABLE THRESHOLDS

One uncertainty implied in the evaluation of past variables or ratios, is the lack of defined thresholds applicable to most countries, dividing ratios of acceptable risks from unacceptable risks. That should not be surprising.

There are wide differences among countries in their willingness to make sacrifices in order to pay external debts. Some countries go to great lengths to pay external debts, while others take a much more relaxed attitude about it. It can be, for instance, hardly a coincidence that by 1937 none of the foreign bonds issued in the United States during the 1920s by Western and Northern Europe and Far Eastern borrowers were in default, while 72 percent of the Latin American issues were in default.[2]

On the other hand, one should keep in mind that while the current account of a country is in deficit—as most of them are—the funds needed to repay external debts which become due do not come from foreign exchange earnings but from rollover credit facilities, or from new financing. In essence the loan servicing depends on subsequent judgments about the borrower's creditworthiness, which may change over time.

As a result there are no general thresholds which indicate whether and when payment difficulties may arise.

The reader will find a few indicative thresholds listed in Chapter 9 under "Indicative Thresholds".

The lack of well-defined thresholds is generally overcome by using ranking systems that show which countries have above or below average ratios (see Chapter 11, under "Ranking Systems and Relative Indicators").

VALIDITY OF EVALUATION OVER TIME

There is also the problem of time limitation for the validity of forecasts on which the creditworthiness evaluation is based. Benjamin Weiner states " . . . one cannot, as a rule, make political forecasts far ahead of time, say beyond three years. Beyond that is fantasy. . . ."[3]

The repayment of bond issues is of course well beyond that limit, and so is, unfortunately, international bank lending.

There is no basic difference between domestic and international banking relationships. Both involve extending credit on an indefinite revolving basis which goes well beyond a three-year period. There is no such thing as "hit and

---

[2]Ilse Mintz. *Deterioration in the Quality of Foreign Bonds Issued in the United States 1920–1930.* National Bureau of Economic Research, Inc., New York, New York, 1951; Table 17, p. 94.
[3]Benjamin Weiner. *Assessing Country Risk.* Euromoney Publications, London, 1981; Chapter 16, New Factors in Country Risk Analysis: Separatism and Religion, p. 135.

run" banking where a bank extends a short-term loan, collects interest and principal, and closes the relationship. There is either a continuing bank/client relationship or there is no regular banking. Short-term lending is mostly an illusion.

STATE OF THE ART

Several difficulties arise when trying to summarize the state of the art of international creditworthiness evaluation systems.

Published material is limited; therefore, the survey of the state of the art has to be based mainly on procedures followed by various lenders, mostly commercial banks.

Some banks prefer not to give information on their evaluation systems; others give a generic outline of their procedures. It is fair to assume that many banks consider their more sophisticated models, on which they have spent considerable time and money, as some kind of trade secret, not to be disclosed to outsiders.

Manfred Kraffczyk describes well the situation: " . . . the evaluation scheme of any one bank is intended to match or, preferably, outperform those of its competitors."[4]

Recent developments have generated doubts about the effectiveness of past country evaluation procedures and have prompted some banks to revise their procedures; one gets the impression that banks are more reluctant than ever to give information on the subject to third parties.

At any rate, country evaluation procedures have been evolving over time (see Chapter 9, STRUCTURED SYSTEMS' OUTLINES AND MODELS).

More than 110 banks were contacted in order to obtain information about their evaluation procedures, 40 in the United States and 70 abroad. Twenty gave information.

The state of the art of country evaluation is discussed in chapters 5, 6, 7, 8 and 9, which contain summaries and critical evaluations of the basic concepts underlying systems currently in use and report practical methods and procedures followed by banks for creditworthiness assessment.

A PRIVATE LENDER'S APPROACH

Country analyses are made for different purposes. The viewpoint of a private lender is different from that of an official lender or from the viewpoint of a corporation considering a direct investment abroad.

---

[4]Manfred Kraffczyk. "Evaluation of Country Risks," Presentation given in Waco, Texas, November 1980.

Official lenders act mainly on the basis of political and/or social consid-erations, which are of secondary importance to private lenders. Official attitudes influence, of course, the thinking of private lenders; but one should keep in mind that sometimes the aims of official entities may actually conflict with the best interests of private lenders.

Corporations considering a direct investment in a country, on the other hand, take a long range view. They are more concerned with the economic growth of a country than with its external repayment capabilities.

chapter 4

What Is the Analyst Looking For?

Robert Z. Aliber states: "The first proposition is that the external debt of the developing countries will not be repaid, in the aggregate, any more than the AT&T debt will be repaid or the Canadian debt will be repaid. The debts of individual countries generally will be repaid as they mature. At the same time, the countries will be borrowing abroad, so, in effect, the funds obtained from the new debt will be used to pay off the maturing debt."[1]

A factual confirmation is found in Volume 32 of the *Balance of Payments Statistics* (BPS), published by the IMF. Of 112 countries for which balance of payments data are published, 90 countries show an overall current account deficit for the last five years reported (1976 to 1980).

It is therefore reasonable to accept Stephen H. Goodman's statement that: "The issue is not whether the developing countries will be able to repay their debt, but rather whether they will continue to be able to service their debt— that is to pay interest—and to roll over the principal on their existing debt and arrange additional financing."[2]

[1]Robert Z. Aliber. "Financing and Risk in Developing Countries." In *Proceedings of a Symposium on Developing Countries' Debt.* Sponsored by the Export-Import Bank of the United States, August 1977; Chapter 7, Panel Discussion: Private Bank Lending and the Debt Situation of the Developing Countries, p. 64.
[2]Stephen H. Goodman. "Financing and Risk in Developing Countries." In *Proceedings of a Symposium on Developing Countries' Debt.* Sponsored by the Export-Import Bank of the United States, August 1977; Introduction: An Overview of Financing and Risk in Developing Countries, p. 3.

The reader should note the distinction between payment of interest—which is an expenditure and as such comes out of income—and payment of principal—which comes out of rollovers or additional financing.

Since principal will not be repaid in the foreseeable future, the analyst should focus his attention on the basic performance of a country rather than on its liquidity problems. The main problem is to identify symptoms of over-indebtedness and/or poor export performance; liquidity cannot be disregarded but should be relegated to second place.

FOREIGN EXCHANGE GENERATING CAPABILITY

The second proposition is that external debts can be repaid only with foreign exchange.

Although the international accounts of a country are only an extension of the domestic economy, one should keep in mind that an increase of Gross Domestic Product (GDP) helps external creditors only if it is accompanied by an increase of foreign exchange earnings. GDP increases should not be automatically accepted as an indicator of improved repayment capability.

A country's rapid economic development with concurrent heavy external borrowing is similar to a rapid expansion of a business enterprise financed by an ever-expanding debt. Over-expansion is one of the most common causes of business failure and, similarly, of international payment difficulties.

One should, therefore, examine closely a country's foreign exchange generating capability, and the rate of increase of the earnings and their vulnerability to exogenous factors such as reduction in price and demand of key exports.

OVERSPENDING ABROAD

At home a government may overspend almost indefinitely by borrowing on domestic markets and monetizing whatever it is unable to borrow, but it cannot do so abroad.

The balance of payments in the current account shows whether a country is spending abroad more than it is earning. The imbalance of the current account indicates the extent of the overspending. A comparison of the current account deficit with total foreign exchange earnings indicates the degree of the problem created by overspending. A comparison of current account deficits with foreign exchange earning increases gives an indication of whether foreign exchange earnings are keeping up with the burden imposed by new external debts (see

Chapter 14, THE CURRENT ACCOUNT and Chapter 15, GROSS EXTER-
NAL REVENUES (GER)).

BURDEN IMPOSED BY EXTERNAL OBLIGATIONS ON FOREIGN EXCHANGE EARNINGS

The importance of determining the relative burden imposed on the foreign
exchange earnings of a country by the payment of interest due on external debts
should be obvious. Payment of interest is a priority obligation which preempts
foreign exchange earnings and which cannot be neglected if a country does not
want to run the risk of having its sources of foreign capital dry up.

On the other hand, some countries have substantial foreign exchange reserves and other fixed income producing assets abroad, and their income should
be deducted from interest payable to foreigners in order to calculate the net
burden caused by the imbalance between debit and credit items.

Direct equity investments of foreigners are quite substantial in some countries, and the remittance abroad of their earnings may cause a considerable
burden on external revenues and should therefore be taken into consideration.
Most developing countries have only insignificant or no equity investments
abroad, but any income from such investments should be taken into account.

The best source of information about external interest and dividend payments is the "investment income" section of the balance of payments which
reports external financial expenditures and income (see Chapter 16, FINAN-
CIAL INCOME AND EXPENDITURES).

EXTERNAL REPAYMENT CAPABILITY INDICATOR

Poor foreign exchange earnings performance, bad external overspending habits,
and heavy external indebtedness are the most common causes of external payment difficulties and as such should represent fundamental elements in the
creditworthiness evaluation.

Therefore, the three elements are combined for the purposes of this study
to calculate a country's "external repayment capability indicator" as keystone of
the creditworthiness evaluation (see Chapter 11, under "External Repayment
Capability"). The creditworthiness of any country with relatively poor repayment
capability should be looked at with suspicion.

The validity of the repayment capability concept is tested in Chapter 19,
EXPERIMENTAL TESTING—CONCLUSIONS, where Factual Repayment
Risk indicators are calculated for 47 countries on the basis of data available before

the Mexican payment difficulties. It is interesting that most of the Latin American big spenders are at the bottom of the list: Venezuela, Chile, Ecuador, Mexico, Bolivia, Brazil, and Costa Rica (in descending order).

LIQUIDITY PROBLEMS

The traditional approach to the examination of liquidity problems is discussed in Chapter 4, LIQUIDITY PROBLEMS. It consists mostly of an examination of reserves and of various reserve–related ratios.

One of the common causes of liquidity crises is bunching of maturities. When lenders are uncertain about the advisability of extending credit, they usually insist upon short-term maturities. That is, of course, self–defeating because it inevitably creates bunching problems which frequently lead to reschedulings.

Two liquidity indicators, not based on reserves and not commonly used, are discussed in Chapter 11, under Liquidity Problems. They are:

— interest earned on international assets as percentage of interest due on external debt, and
— balances of a country and its residents with banks reporting to the Bank for International Settlements (BIS) as percent of the amounts due by each country and its residents to the same banks.

PER CAPITA INCOME INCREASES—POPULATION INCREASES

In the absence of better indicators, "per capita income increases" and "population increases" could be used as long-range indirect political instability indicators.

With the exception of countries where petroleum production or the production of other commodities represent a substantial share of GDP, per capita income is the best indicator of a country's economic sophistication (the subject is discussed in Chapter 17, under "Per Capita Income").

Population increases are one of the most intractable problems of developing countries. High birth rates not only cause the immediate problem of feeding and sheltering an increasing population, their effect is felt 15 or 20 years later when additional jobs will have to be found for the new entrants into the labor force.

DOMESTIC CURRENCY PURCHASING POWER CHANGES

This subject is discussed in Chapter 12, PRIVATE BORROWERS.

Changes in a currency's purchasing power parity may cause the currency to become overvalued and thus adversely affect a country's export earnings.

Such currency purchasing power changes are particularly dangerous to private borrowers because they usually lead to substantial currency devaluations which may cause an unbearable debt servicing burden on private borrowers.

SOCIAL AND POLITICAL FACTORS

The past performance of a country is the result of the interaction of its underlying social, political, and economic structure and institutions, and of the priorities followed by its government. All favorable, or unfavorable, factors are included and weighed in the performance reflected by the economic statistics of a country.

If statistics indicate a relatively moderate amount of external debts and show a steady growth of foreign exchange earnings or other signs indicating that the external accounts are in good order, the prospective lender will know that the overall structure and institutions of a country have evolved in a way that is favorable to the external creditor.

To quantify social, political, and economic institutions for creditworthiness evaluation purposes is a subjective process which may, and one would expect should, lead to different evaluations as made by different individuals. Intangible factors should not be quantified because the procedure conveys the impression of a scientific precision which, in fact, does not exist.

Pages may be written, for instance, about a country's "degree of development and diversification of the economy," or its "current account adjustment policies," but their meaning insofar as creditworthiness is concerned will seldom be un-equivocal. On the other hand, a resulting good export performance or reasonable level of external indebtedness are unequivocally good creditworthiness signs. One should, therefore, analyze results rather than causes.

SUGGESTED APPROACH

A review of international creditworthiness analysis systems presently in use indicates that most of them consist of studies in depth, supplemented by statistical data (see Chapter 9, STRUCTURED SYSTEMS' OUTLINES AND MODELS).

It is suggested that the procedure should be reversed, that the assessment should be based mainly on comparable facts complemented by noncomparable facts and subjective judgments. In other words, one should first determine whether the comparative past performance justifies the granting of credit to a country or its nationals, and then one should try to forecast future economic and political developments.

The report submitted to management should reflect the procedure followed for the evaluation and should consist of four sections:

— Comparable Factual Data
— Judgmental Economic Factors

— Judgmental Social and Political Factors
— Conclusions.

This arrangement shows to what extent the evaluation is based on comparable data, or on judgmental assessments of noncomparable factors.

The factors to be included in the Comparable Factual Data section are:

— relative external repayment capability
— relative liquidity
— relative per capita income increase and population increase
— relative currency overvaluation.

The concepts underlying the compilation of this section are discussed in Chapters 11 to 17.

Some experimental applications of the suggested procedures and some examples of comparable factual risk profiles are reported in Chapter 19, EXPERIMENTAL TESTING—CONCLUSIONS.

No overall creditworthiness ranking calculations are attempted in this study because no satisfactory weighing system has been found for factual data and no satisfactory quantification system has been found for social and political factors.

II

State of the Art

chapter 5

Growth-Cum-Debt Theories

The traditional country creditworthiness analysis is based on economic growth theories. The basic concept is that foreign equity capital and money borrowed abroad supplement national resources and thus increase capital formation, which in turn accelerates the rate of economic growth.

The use of economic growth concepts for creditworthiness analysis purposes rests on the fundamental assumption ". . . that continuing growth in per-capita production and the underlying process of rapid accumulation of productive capital is the basic long-run condition of debt servicing capacity."[1] One should note that the Avramovic study is the result of the collective efforts of the staff of the Economic Department of the World Bank. One should also note that the World Bank is more interested in the economic development of a country than in its external creditworthiness.

Growth-cum-debt theories imply some kind of overall investment program instead of a sequence of mostly unrelated, incidental loans, as is common banking practice.

Economic growth is generally desirable, but it is relevant to private lenders only if it is accompanied by an increase of foreign exchange earnings.

---

[1]Dragoslav Avramovic, et al. *Economic Growth and External Debt.* Published for the World Bank by The Johns Hopkins University Press, Baltimore, Maryland, 1964; Chapter 2, Conceptual Framework, p. 11.

THE RESOURCES GAP

The first step in determining the relevance of macroeconomic development theories to external creditworthiness analysis is to find out to what extent international lending is actually connected with economic development.

A growth-cum-debt situation is caused by a "resources gap," namely by a failure of domestic savings to fund investments. The country will have to borrow the difference abroad and the disequilibrium will show up in the external accounts as an imbalance in the balance of payments in the current account. That does not automatically indicate however whether the deficit in current account is due to exogenous causes, such as a reduction in demand or price of some

Table 1   Current Account Imbalance as Percentage of the Total of Gross Fixed Capital Formation plus Current Account Imbalance—Average 1978–1980.

Malta	Cred.	68.5	Mexico	14.1
So. Africa	Cred.	23.2	Guatemala	14.4
Switzerland	Cred.	11.3	Egypt	14.6
Indonesia	Cred.	6.7	Tunisia	15.3
Malaysia	Cred.	4.7	Greece	15.9
Colombia	Cred.	4.6	So. Korea	16.6
United Kingdom	Cred.	2.1	Philippines	17.4
Italy	Cred.	.9	Brazil	17.5
Japan		.1	Paraguay	17.8
France		.7	Ireland	19.1
United States		.8	Israel	19.6
Spain		1.2	Thailand	20.4
Germany		2.4	Pakistan	21.1
Venezuela		2.8	Ecuador	21.3
Finland		3.0	Jamaica	24.5
Iceland		4.2	Zambia	24.5
Norway		5.2	Cyprus	25.2
Canada		5.8	Sri Lanka	26.3
Netherlands		6.2	Bolivia	27.0
Syria		11.1	Morocco	28.3
Sweden		11.3	Chile	28.5
Austria		11.6	Honduras	29.5
New Zealand		12.1	Kenya	32.5
Australia		12.2	Tanzania	33.1
Belgium		12.9	Costa Rica	34.4
Turkey		13.2		

Source: *International Financial Statistics* (IFS), December 1981.

commodities exported, or to excess consumption, or to the government's investment policies.

One could attempt to detect an underlying resources gap and to measure its relative size by comparing the external capital inflows of a country with its total investments. That means the ratio Current Account Imbalance as Percentage of the Total of Gross Fixed Capital Formation Plus Current Account Imbalance.

On the basis of that ratio, one could determine which countries obtained abroad a higher share of the funds needed for development and assume that the external borrowings of those countries is mainly development related.

Table 1 shows how much of a country's investment funds came from abroad. The sample consists of 51 countries and the period covered is 1978 to 1980. A three-year period is selected because it is fairly recent and gives an idea of the basic situation.

Eight countries included in the sample had overall credit balances in current account during the three-year period. Four of them are developing countries: Colombia, Indonesia, Malaysia, and Malta.

It would be arbitrary to select a ratio as a dividing line between countries borrowing mostly for developing purposes from those borrowing for other purposes. One may, however, assume that a higher share of the money borrowed abroad is used for economic development in countries with a higher ratio of current account deficit to invested funds.

THE AVRAMOVIC MODEL

According to Avramovic, the crucial variables ". . . return on capital, savings, investment, growth of output, required foreign capital inflow and the associated cycles of debt service ratios—should be formulated and their time-paths followed."[2]

Unfortunately he does not mention the foreign exchange generating capability of a country among the crucial variables. At any rate, the influence of the Avramovic school of thought should not be underestimated, so that a closer look at his models is advisable.

The Liquidity Aspect

To judge the size and gravity of payment problems which debtor countries may encounter if external receipts suddenly fall, Avramovic considers the following factors:[3]

[2]Ibid., Chapter 2, Conceptual Framework, pp. 11–12.
[3]Ibid., Chapter 3, The Liquidity Aspect of Debt Servicing Capacity, p. 13.

1. Fluctuating variables (disturbance variables)
   a. exports
   b. capital flows
   c. emergency and inflation-induced imports
2. Offsetting variables (compensating variables)
   a. reserves
   b. compensatory finance
   c. compressible imports
3. Rigid variables
   a. minimum tolerable imports
   b. debt service—interest
   c. debt service—amortization

The practical usefulness of the model is doubtful. For instance, future capital inflow is anybody's guess; moreover, "emergency and inflation-induced imports," "compressible imports," and "minimum tolerable imports" are only guestimates. The last two items are based on the concept that nonessential or luxury consumption could be eliminated or at least reduced. The problem is that in consumer societies any existing consumption becomes essential. For instance: Are the luxury goods imported to satisfy the demands of foreign tourists essential? Is the bulletproof limousine for the head of the state more "essential" than the caviar for foreign tourists?

If the model is to be practically useful, the bureaucrat who decides these issues should follow the standards used by the analyst—and that is highly improbable.

It would seem that under present-day conditions, a country's imports, like its government's expenditures, are subject to the inverse of the law of gravity: there is a relentless force pushing them up. As in gravity, the force increases with the mass. One should remember C. Northcote Parkinson's law: Expenditure rises to meet income. That should probably be updated to read: Expenditure rises to meet at least 115 percent of income.

The Long-Term Aspect

Avramovic points out that the macroeconomic benefits of foreign capital depend on:

A. The efficiency with which resources, including foreign capital, are translated into income.

B.   The extent to which the additional income stream is saved and used to finance domestic investment and/or public development expenditure.

C.   The rapidity with which internal structural adjustments are made and then reflected in the composition of imports and exports.[4]

But such intangible factors cannot be worked into a model, as shown by the following variables included in his "single generation" variant of the model:

A.   "Income growth target" — indicating the desired rate of increase in GDP.

B.   "Savings rates" — an assumed domestic savings rate is indicated.

C.   "Capital-output ratio" — an assumed ratio is selected; for instance, a 3 : 1 ratio indicates that a unit of gross capital input yields to the national economy 33 percent in terms of gross value added.

D.   "Export coefficient" — proportion of export earnings to total income.

E.   "Export growth rate" — an assumed growth rate.

F.   "Foreign capital" — initial debt is assumed to be zero; further assumption is that gross borrowing takes place without interruption in amounts required to bridge the savings-investment gap and to cover debt service payments.

G.   "Debt service" — an assumed interest rate is used to estimate the servicing, with an assumed average maturity of the loan.[5]

The numerical illustration of the "single generation" variant leads to a debt cycle span of 36 years; that is, of course, of little interest to commercial banks. Bank lending during the last decade was mostly for recycling OPEC surplus to other countries. There was no dividing line for the allocation of funds for various purposes, such as productive investments, non-productive investments, or consumption expenditures. All the funds went into one pot.

The fundamental difficulty with the model is the essentially arbitrary nature of the assumptions on which it rests. The model disregards exogenous factors and global inflationary trends. It assumes a long-term fixed capital-output rate and a long-term fixed export coefficient.

One may add that a creditworthiness evaluation is really not necessary if foreign credit, as assumed in the "single generation" variant, will be available

4Ibid., Chapter 5, The Long-Term Aspect of Debt Servicing Capacity, under, Macro-Economic Costs and Their Time-Sequence, p. 53.
5Ibid., Chapter 5, The Long-Term Aspect of Debt Servicing Capacity, under, The Model and Its Assumptions—"Single Generation" Variant, pp. 57–59.

". . . without interruption in the amount required to bridge the savings-invest-ment gap and to cover debt service payments."[6]

Avramovic is, of course, well aware of the imperfections of the model. In the conclusions he states: "This study has not solved the debt servicing problems, nor has it succeeded in identifying one or a few statistical indicators which would conclusively show that the limits of indebtedness at conventional terms have been reached. Rather, it has arrived at a negative conclusion that such indicators probably do not exist."[7]

THE TECHNOLOGICAL GAP

How effective external borrowing turns out to be in accelerating a country's economic growth depends on many human factors which a model cannot take into consideration because they cannot be quantified.

A model cannot reflect the importance of technology or of the entrepre-neurial spirit. Avramovic mentioned in 1964 that "Fifteen years ago, economic forecasts for these countries (Japan and Italy) were not too exuberant, in view of the structural problems whose solution seemed to require a very long time. The forecasters certainly did not envisage the impressive record of growth and structural change which has been attained in less than one-half of the lifetime of a single generation.[8] What the forecasters missed was existing technological know-how and a strong desire to repair war damages and return to normal life.

Perhaps one of the reasons why so many economists seem to believe that injections of money will automatically accelerate economic growth is the success of the Marshall Plan. Compared to the GDP of the recipient countries, the funds transferred were relatively small (probably about 2 percent) but the results were dramatic. The reason is that the knowledge and experience required to run industrial economies were already there. The bridges, railroads, and factories had been destroyed, but the bombings did not destroy technological knowledge and experience. It was only a matter of giving the recipients the missing foreign exchange working capital to get them started.

That, unfortunately, is not the case for most developing countries where, together with the problem of rapidly rising populations, one of the biggest prob-lems is lack of technology. It seems to be often forgotten that it takes 16 years of schooling before an individual graduates from college. But college graduates are not enough; a whole pyramid of skills, from mechanics to experienced

[6]Ibid., Chapter 5, The Long-Term Aspect of Debt Servicing Capacity, under, The Model and Its Assumptions—"Single Generation" Variant, p. 59.

[7]Ibid., Chapter 6, Conclusions, p. 94.

[8]Ibid., Chapter 5, The Long-Term Aspect of Debt Servicing Capacity, under, The Extremes, p. 56.

executives, is needed to run an industrial economy. Foreign technical know-how could be hired. But many emerging nations are highly suspicious of foreign technicians. Xenophobic barriers are a delicate subject, and not only in developing countries. They may considerably retard a country's economic development.

GDP OR GNP DENOMINATORS

The widespread use of GDP or GNP denominators in international creditworthiness evaluations is based on the assumption that a higher GDP enhances a country's external repayment capabilities.

P. Henry Mueller, for instance, warns that ". . . one must be careful to avoid the simple cash flow type of analysis."[9] He states that ". . . on the foreign exchange side, a government has almost unlimited power to accumulate necessary exchange for debt servicing. First, a government has at its disposal monetary and fiscal policy, as well as other instruments to promote balance of payments equilibrium. Moreover, restrictions on payments for imports are a common control imposed by governments to assure they have adequate foreign exchange income from available sources for debt servicing. Another major technique used for this purpose, but often not well understood, is adjustment in exchange rates. Even without direct controls, there will always be an exchange rate which will equilibrate supply and demand for foreign exchange (including demand for foreign exchange for debt servicing) if a central bank decides to achieve such equilibrium."[10]

Z. A. Aliber, however, observes "in this sense (to squeeze a surplus from their residents) the authorities might be considered to have an option—although if they exercise the option, they may no longer be the authorities."[11]

One should also note that government policies do not affect exogenous conditions; they do not increase demand or prices of commodities or other goods exported by a country. They cannot remedy structural export weaknesses.

The importance attributed by lenders to the GDP factor is confirmed by H. Robert Heller's simple lagged cross-country regression calculations. He found that "The coefficient shows that for every dollar increase in GDP, total external debt tends to increase by approximately 19 cents."[12] Heller also tested the re-

[9]P. Henry Mueller. *Offshore Lending by U.S. Commercial Banks*. Bankers' Association for Foreign Trade, Washington, D.C. and Robert Morris Associates, Philadelphia, Pa., 1981; Chapter 1, A Conspectus for Offshore Lenders, p. 22.

[10]Ibid., pp. 21–22.

[11]Z. A. Aliber. "Living with Developing Country Debt," Lloyds Bank Review, October 1977, p. 43.

[12]H. Robert Heller. "International Lending, Risk, and Portfolio Quality." Conference on the Conditions for International Stability, Montevideo, Uruguay, December 1981, p. 12.

Table 2   Gross External Revenues* as Percentage of GDP--1978/1980

Belgium	68.3	Germany	28.8
Ireland	65.7	Indonesia	28.8
Israel	65.0	Costa Rica	27.8
Malaysia	59.1	France	26.7
Netherlands	56.5	New Zealand	25.9
Cyprus	54.9	Ecuador	25.8
Jamaica	54.9	Egypt	25.4
Norway	46.3	Guatemala	24.7
Iceland	44.2	Thailand	24.6
Switzerland	41.9	Morocco	24.2
Zambia	40.4	Greece	22.7
Honduras	40.2	Philippines	22.4
Sri Lanka	39.8	Chile	22.1
Tunisia	38.5	Pakistan	22.0
Austria	37.2	Tanzania	18.8
So. Korea	36.4	Bolivia	18.3
So. Africa	36.0	Colombia	17.7
Finland	33.3	Australia	17.5
Venezuela	33.2	Paraguay	17.3
Syria	33.1	Spain	16.7
United Kingdom	32.9	United States	14.1
Sweden	31.5	Japan	13.3
Kenya	30.4	Mexico	12.5
Canada	29.7	Brazil	8.8
Italy	28.9	Turkey	8.7

*See Chapter 15, GROSS EXTERNAL REVENUES (GER)
Source: *Balance of Payments Statistics* (BPS), Vol. 32 *International Financial Statistics* (IFS), December 1981.

lationship between imports and total external debt, and between exports and total external debt. He found that "Considering all three factors—GDP—imports and exports—we find that GDP is by far the best explanatory variable for a country's total bank debt level."[13]

Heller's calculations confirm the widespread use of GDP standards for external creditworthiness evaluation purposes.

The use of GDP as common denominator for external repayment capability comparisons would be justified if all of the GDP were automatically convertible into foreign exchange, or if, at least, a fairly constant relationship existed between each country's GDP and its foreign exchange earnings. But, of course, that is not the case.

[13]Ibid., p. 13.

Table 2 shows "Gross External Revenues (GER) as Percentage of GDP" for a sample of 50 countries for the years 1978 to 1980. Gross External Revenues are discussed in Chapter 15, GROSS EXTERNAL REVENUES (GER). They include all foreign exchange earned plus unrequited transfers.

Some readers may be surprised to see that on the basis of the foreign exchange component in the GDP, export-oriented Japan is close to the bottom of the list.

The gross external revenues (GER) to GDP ratios of the countries included in the sample vary from a low of 8.7 percent for Turkey to a high of 68.3 percent for Belgium. An almost eightfold variation in the GER to GDP relationship clearly indicates how misleading it could be to use a country's GDP as an external repayment capability measuring standard.

One of the weaknesses of GDP ratios, insofar as international creditworthiness evaluation is concerned, is that the ratios of countries with large populations are artificially favorable because the countries have a large GDP. The following example concerning two countries with widely different total population illustrates the point:

1978–1980 (three–year total in billion SDRs)	Brazil	Denmark
Deficit in current account	23.61	5.44
Gross Domestic Product (GDP)	502.23	147.40
Gross External Revenues (GER)	43.99	49.81
Current Account Deficit as percentage of:		
GDP	4.7%	3.7%
GER	53.7%	10.9%

Source: *IFS*, December 1981 and *BPS*, Vol. 32.

Although the Current Account Deficits as Percentage of GDP ratios of the two countries are not too far apart, (4.7 and 3.7 percent respectively), Brazil's current account deficit as percentage of the foreign exchange earned is five times higher (53.7 percent) than Denmark's (10.9 percent), reflecting two completely different external repayment capability situations.

Heller's calculations that "for every dollar increase in GDP, total external debt tends to increase by approximately 19 cents" suggest that the use of GDP as measuring standard in appraising a country's creditworthiness was one of the factors which led banks to lend large amounts of money to countries with a large GDP but relatively modest foreign exchange generating capability.

OVER-EXPANSIONARY POLICIES

Over-expansion fueled by borrowing is a frequent cause of financial trouble for business enterprises; that applies also to countries. Government over-expansionary policies, supported by external borrowing, have probably caused more external payment difficulties than shrinking demand or depressed prices of a country's commodity exports.

It is ironic that some credit analysts should be favorably impressed by a rapid expansion of a country's GDP, while the "medicine" almost invariably prescribed by the IMF for external payment difficulties is a slowdown in economic growth.

One may add that GDP increases may reflect import substitution projects which do not add to foreign exchange earnings and may, on the contrary, impose new burdens for raw materials, fuel, or spare parts on the external accounts.

EXCHANGE RATE CHANGES

A secondary reason why the use of the GDP for international creditworthiness ratios should be avoided is that the GDP is expressed in domestic currency, while external debts are in foreign currency, so that comparison may be misleading.

For instance, at the end of 1975 Mexico's external debts were estimated to be about $15 billion; at the then prevailing rate of exchange for the Mexican peso, the external debts were about 19 percent of its GDP. However, as a result of the 1976 peso devaluation, the external debt to GDP ratio jumped to 30 percent. The drastic deterioration of the ratio was meaningless. As a fact, from the viewpoint of the external creditor, the country's creditworthiness improved after the devaluation since the imbalance between domestic and international prices was reduced.

chapter 6

Liquidity Problems

Although most banks differentiate between short-term, medium-term and long-term lending, the distinction is artificial for most of the developing countries whose current accounts are steadily in deficit.

While this condition prevails, overall repayment of loans cannot take place; the lender/borrower relationship becomes one of a permanent nature. Short-term loans have to be regularly rolled over and become in substance long-term, regardless of their formal short-term classification.

Since the relationship is in substance long-term, banks should be mainly concerned with the debtor's long-term performance (see Chapter 4, "WHAT IS THE ANALYST LOOKING FOR?").

Robert Z. Aliber stated in 1977 that ". . . debt reschedulings are an inevitable part of the process because such a large part of the external debt is of such short maturity. Reschedulings, however, are anticipated events, and most lenders are not worse off as a result of reschedulings since the present value of their claims on the developing countries does not decline. Whenever there is a cyclical problem, the lenders become cautious, and, as a consequence, their concern may become self-fulfilling."[1]

What actually counts is the structural ability of a country to carry its external

[1] Robert Z. Aliber. "Financing and Risk in Developing Countries." In *Proceedings of a Symposium on Developing Countries' Debt.* Sponsored by the Export-Import Bank of the United States, August 1977; Chapter7, Panel Discussion: Private Bank Lending and the Debt Situation of the Developing Countries, p. 65.

debt burden in the long-run; nevertheless, liquidity problems should not be ignored.

RESERVES

The indicator most commonly used to analyze liquidity problems is the total of the reserves.

Generally speaking, the function of reserves is to act as a cushion for cyclical variations in a country's external revenues and for emergencies. The reserves do not represent money set aside for payment of external debts; they will be used for payment of all external expenditures.

The size of reserves gives a first indication of the magnitude of the international cash flows of a country and, indirectly, of the size of the international credit that could be carried by the country. For instance, other factors being equal, the repayment potential of a country with reserves in the $4 to $6 billion range should be higher than that of a country whose reserves are at the $400 to $600 million level.

Reserves are used only after all foreign exchange transactions are compensated through the normal international clearing arrangements and after the everyday credit facilities are used. Thus, increases, or decreases, of reserves represent net imbalances of all payments affecting the international liquidity of a country. The variations will indicate the disequilibrium between foreign exchange inflow and outflow.

DEFINITION OF RESERVES

What reserves are is explained in the *Balance of Payments Manual* under "Reserves—Explanation of Concept" paragraph 439:

> " 'Reserves' is singled out as a category because the kind of capital that it is designed to comprise can perform a distinctive and important function in the context of an economy's international transactions. The category may be described as the monetary gold, special drawing rights (SDRs) in the Fund, reserve position in the Fund, use of Fund credit, and existing claims on nonresidents that are available to the central authorities either to finance payments imbalances directly or to manage the size of such imbalances by intervening to influence the exchange rate for the national currency."[2]

The definition seems clear enough, but paragraph 442 of *The Manual* raises a few questions. It states that the financial assets in the reserves "cannot un-

---

[2]*Balance of Payments Manual, Fourth Edition,* International Monetary Fund, 1977; Chapter 21, Reserves, (1) Explanation of Concept, p. 147.

ambiguously be identified" and that "the readily observable characteristics of a claim are not sufficient to establish whether a claim is actually available to the central authorities" to be used as reserves.

Moreover, paragraph 442 also states that

". . . assets that are pledged, committed, earmarked, set aside in sinking funds, blocked, sold forward, or otherwise encumbered by their holder are nonetheless existing assets and are not precluded on these grounds alone from forming part of the reserves."[3]

The last sentence of paragaph 442 is in obvious contradiction with paragraph 439. If assets that are pledged, committed, earmarked, set aside in sinking funds, blocked, sold forward, or otherwise encumbered, are nonetheless included in the reserves, then some of the reserves are obviously not available for the purposes for which they are intended: "to finance payments imbalances." The analyst can only hope that the bulk of the reserves is not encumbered by their holders.

COMPOSITION OF RESERVES

Reserves are reported in the *International Financial Statistics* (IFS) under "International Liquidity" as:

Total Reserves, minus Gold

—SDRs

—Reserve Position in the Fund

—Foreign Exchange

Gold (Million Fine Troy Ounces)

Gold (National Valuation).[4]

As to their composition, one may point out that they include earned money (foreign exchange), reserve "assets" which are not earned (SDRs and Reserve position in the Fund), and a commodity (gold).

Objections against the use of reserves as performance indicators for creditworthiness evaluation purposes, may be summarized:

— ambiguities mentioned in paragraph 442 of *The Manual*;

— a country may be accumulating heavy external debts and still show satisfactory reserves trends;

---

[3]Ibid., Chapter 21, Reserves, (2) Coverage of Foreign Exchange Assets, p. 148.
[4]*International Financial Statistics* (hereafter cited as *IFS*).

— allocations of quotas (reserve position in the Fund) and SDRs are not earned and, therefore, do not reflect performance;

— uncertainties about the evaluation of gold included in the reserves, and

— uncertainty as to whether, and to what extent, gold holdings are marketable and the proceeds of their sale readily available to the authorities for the purposes for which reserves are held.

ACCUMULATION OF EXTERNAL DEBTS AND LEVEL OF RESERVES

The main weakness of reserves as a performance indicator is that the country may be going deeply into debt and still show steadily increasing reserves.

A case in point is Mexico, which had been running deficits in the current account for 20 consecutive years before the 1976 devaluation. Yet its reserves were remarkably stable, increasing gradually from the $400 to $500 million level in the mid 1950s to $1.5 billion at the end of 1975.

Moreover, a new phenomenon appeared in the second half of the 1970s. Non-oil exporting developing countries started accumulating reserves while their current accounts were in deficit.

Jack Guenther estimates that "In 1978, when there was a deficit to be financed of $20 billion, they (non-oil developing countries) actually accumulated reserves of $18 billion: their net borrowing was $39 billion."[5]

Perhaps some developing countries were making a profit by borrowing at low interest rates from official institutions while earning a high return on their reserves.

A quick comparison of some of the 1976 and 1978 reserves figures shows that the reserves of the following countries more than doubled, *while their current account was in deficit* during the years 1977/78:

Reserves	(Million of dollars) 12/31/76	12/31/78	Percentage Change
Paraguay	158	466	Plus 195%
Ghana	104	287	Plus 176%
Costa Rica	98	198	Plus 102%
Source: IFS, July 1979; BPS, Vol. 31.			

[5]Jack Guenther. *Assessing Country Risk.* Euromoney Publications, London, 1981; Chapter 20, The Outlook for the 1980s, pp. 157–158.

It should be obvious that satisfactory reserves trends do not necessarily indicate that a country's international performance is good: they only mean that a country could borrow abroad if and when it wanted to. (See Chapter 13, under "Aggregate Presentation.")

ALLOCATION OF SDR'S AND FUND QUOTAS

Another problem, if one wants to use reserves as a performance indicator, is caused by the allocation of SDRs and Fund "quotas," which determine the "Reserve Position in the Fund."

The allocations are uneven. They are based on a formula that takes into account, among other things, the GDP of a country. Not only are they uneven, they are out of line with the country's international business, which reserves are intended to help finance. For instance, the end of 1979 quotas, as percentage of total foreign exchange earnings, varied from 1.3 percent for Germany to 10.1 percent for India.

In view of the uneven allocation of Fund quotas and SDRs, time series comparisons of reserves are unreliable performance indicators.

EVALUATION AND LIQUIDITY OF GOLD HOLDINGS

The big question is the evaluation of gold holdings included in the reserves. The experts want gold demonetized, dead and forgotten. But the general public does not share the experts' opinion. When the "gold pool" was dissolved in March 1968, the monetary authorities announced that they would neither buy nor sell gold to private holders. As a result, the free market price of gold started moving away from the official price. At the beginning of 1972, when the official price was $38 per ounce, the market price reached the $45 level. In February 1973 when the official price was raised to $40.22, the free market price was in the $80 range and on the way up.

For all practical purposes, official gold holdings became frozen assets. The monetary authorities could not sell to private holders at the market price and would not sell to other official authorities at a price well below market levels. Some countries pledged their gold for external loans. Gold was as liquid as the Crown Jewels.

All along the IMF continued bravely to evaluate official gold holdings in the *IFS* at the official price. Only in August 1979, after the London price of gold had gone over $300 per ounce, did the IMF finally stop evaluating gold held in reserves at 35 SDRs an ounce. With pleasing propriety, it skipped over the problem of the price at which official gold holdings should be evaluated by reporting in the *IFS* "Total Reserves Minus Gold" and adding the items "Gold (Million Fine Troy Ounces)" and "Gold (National Valuation)."

Today, no one knows what to do about the evaluation of official gold holdings, and no one knows whether gold could really be used in large quantities for the purposes for which reserves are held.

The determination of the amount of the reserves has become a matter of opinion. Sometimes the methods that can be used lead to widely conflicting conclusions.

For the United States, the March 1983 *IFS* reported for December 1982:

— 22.81 billion dollars "Total Reserves, Minus Gold"
— 264.3 "Gold (Million Fine Troy Ounces)"
— 11.15 billion dollars "Gold (National Valuation)"

Although bureaucrats at times act in mysterious ways, it is hardly conceivable that they would sell gold at the "national valuation," which at that time was less than one tenth of the market price.

The value to be attributed to the total United States reserves at the end of 1982 is strictly a matter of opinion. One could rationalize any evaluation between $34 billion, with gold at national valuation, and $143 billion, with gold at the London market price of $456.90 an ounce.

GOLD SWAPS

Some of the problems caused by the uncertainty of evaluation and doubtful liquidity of gold have been solved with gold swaps. In substance, foreign exchange is lent against gold collateral.

Typically, the loan is for 75 percent of the market value of the gold and the swap usually runs for six months. A dozen countries have made swaps and the practice will no doubt become more widespread.

That means that a new problem arises for the analyst. In accordance with paragraph 442 of *The Manual*,[6] reserve data published in the *IFS* do not indicate whether any and how much of the gold held in the reserves has been pledged against swaps.

COMPARATIVE ADEQUACY OF RESERVES

While the question of the evaluation and liquidity of the official gold holdings remains unresolved, comparisons of the "adequacy" of the reserves held by each country, made on the basis of their amount, may be quite misleading because

---

[6]*Balance of Payments Manual.* Chapter 21, Reserves, (2) Coverage of Foreign Exchange Assets, p. 148.

of the uneven distribution of gold. Some European countries, for instance, have large gold holdings. At the end of 1982, Italy had more gold than the total held by Canada, Japan, and the United Kingdom combined. Portugal had more gold than the total held by Australia, New Zealand, and South Africa combined. Among the oil-exporting countries, 25 percent held more than 60 percent of the gold. The concentration is even worse among non-oil-exporting developing countries: five countries held more than one half of the total gold.[7]

The analyst should also note that beginning with 1979, Belgium, Denmark, France, Germany, Ireland, Italy, Luxembourg, the Netherlands, and the United Kingdom, participating in the European Monetary Cooperation Fund (EMCF), were issued European Currency Units (ECUs) against their deposits with EMCF of gold and United States dollars. The gold deposited with the EMCF is excluded from the countries' gold holdings and included in foreign exchange, at the EMCF's valuation, at a market–related price. Gold is valued quarterly on the basis of the average of London market prices in the preceeding six months or the average price of the penultimate working day of the period, whichever is lower.

RESERVES TO IMPORTS RATIO

Ratios indicating reserves adequacy are usually expressed as International Reserves to Imports or Months-of-imports Coverage ratios. The first ratio indicates reserves as percentage of yearly imports; the second indicates how many months of average imports are covered by reserves.

Apart from the uncertainty about reserves evaluations, the ratio suffers from lack of precision as to what is meant by the word *imports*. Some texts specify *imports c.i.f.*; others indicate *imports of goods and services*, while frequently only the word *imports* is used.

To include in the ratio only merchandise imports does not make sense because services and debit interest will also have to be paid for. For instance, in Brazil debit interest on external obligations represented 20 percent of all external expenditures during 1980.

Any ratio intended to reflect the relative adequacy of a country's reserves should use "Gross External Expenditures" (GEE) as a measuring standard. That should include all external expenditures for merchandise imported, for services received from foreigners, for debit interest due on external debt, for profits due on equity investments in the country by foreigners, for official expenditures abroad, and, moreover, for official and private unrequited transfers. In other words, all debit entries of the balance of payments in current account (see Chapter 14, under "Gross External Expenditures (GEE)").

[7]March 1983 *IFS.*

CREDIT BALANCES HELD WITH AND AMOUNTS BORROWED FROM BANKS

The quarterly reports prepared by the Bank for International Settlements (BIS) includes a table "External Position of Banks in the Reporting Area and of Certain Offshore Branches of U.S. Banks" (see Chapter 7, under "External Debt Profile"). The table lists the total borrowed by various countries and their residents

Table 3   Credit Balances as Percentage of Amounts Due to Banks Reporting to the Bank for International Settlements (BIS)—September 30, 1981.

	Percent	Relative Indicator (*)		Percent	Relative Indicator (*)
Malta	2,990.9	4548	Italy	57.7	88
Switzerland	527.9	802	Norway	51.1	78
Syria	294.8	447	Germany	48.9	74
Cyprus	192.4	292	Zambia	47.7	72
Netherlands	185.6	282	Ireland	47.1	71
United States	183.6	279	Philippines	46.2	69
Guatemala	163.6	248	Japan	44.7	68
Israel	162.8	247	Thailand	40.7	62
Indonesia	152.7	232	Turkey	39.8	60
Egypt	141.5	215	Chile	38.5	58
Sri Lanka	139.0	211	Finland	38.0	58
United Kingdom	138.1	210	Sweden	31.2	47
Kenya	131.1	199	Costa Rica	26.8	41
Pakistan	126.9	193	Iceland	24.6	37
Paraguay	121.2	184	Bolivia	24.2	37
Malaysia	113.1	172	Australia	21.0	32
France	89.0	135	Ecuador	20.4	31
Tunisia	85.2	129	Honduras	20.4	31
Venezuela	84.1	128	Mexico	20.0	30
Spain	84.0	127	Morocco	18.4	28
Belgium	79.4	120	Jamaica	18.0	27
Canada	75.4	114	New Zealand	17.6	27
Austria	75.0	114	So. Korea	17.4	26
Colombia	73.9	112	So. Africa	16.5	25
Tanzania	72.4	110	Brazil	10.1	15
Greece	65.9	100			

*100 equals median of countries listed, i.e, 65.9.
Source: Bank for International Settlements, Basle, International Banking Developments, February 1982.

from banks in 15 reporting countries (Austria, Belgium, Canada, Denmark, France, West Germany, Ireland, Italy, Japan, Luxembourg, the Netherlands, Sweden, Switzerland, United Kingdom, and United States) and the deposits of each debtor country and its residents with the same banks.

Since the 15 countries include the major banking centers in the world, the data reported should give a fair indication of the credit balances held with banks and of the amounts borrowed from banks by each country and its residents. The relationship between credit balances held by a country and the amounts borrowed by the country from banks is similar to the working capital ratio of a private enterprise; it should be included in the liquidity section of the country report (see Chapter 19, under "Comparable Factual Country Risk Profiles").

Table 3, based on BIS data for the end of September 1981, reports "Credit Balances as Percentage of Amounts due to Banks Reporting to BIS."

Table 4 Fund's Holdings of a Member's Currency as Percentage of the Member's Quota—December 31, 1980.

Malta	47.4	So. Africa	79.8
Paraguay	56.9	Greece	80.0
Colombia	60.5	Chile	80.3
Germany	63.9	Finland	80.3
Austria	65.2	United States	84.7
Italy	65.3	Mexico	87.5
Norway	66.1	Israel	91.7
Ireland	67.1	New Zealand	92.1
Malaysia	69.3	Syria	92.5
France	70.9	Honduras	100.0
Netherlands	71.2	Morocco	100.0
Venezuela	71.3	Jamaica	105.7
Guatemala	71.6	Thailand	108.0
Belgium	72.1	Costa Rica	108.3
Brazil	73.0	Cyprus	108.4
Japan	73.4	Pakistan	109.5
Spain	75.4	Egypt	113.0
Sweden	75.8	Tanzania	117.1
United Kingdom	76.2	Kenya	128.6
Indonesia	77.7	Philippines	132.8
Canada	78.3	Bolivia	133.3
Australia	78.5	Sri Lanka	135.8
Iceland	79.2	So. Korea	152.4
Ecuador	79.3	Turkey	158.3
Tunisia	79.7	Zambia	204.9

Source: *IFS*, February 1981, "Fund Accounts: Position to Date," Column 31.

UTILIZATION OF IMF FACILITIES AS LIQUIDITY INDICATOR

Some analysts use the "percentage of a country's IMF quota utilization" as one of the elements for the evaluation of its international creditworthiness.

The assumption is that a country would use its quota as a last resort; therefore, the use of IMF facilities would indicate that the country has used up its operating funds and has to fall back on its quota in the Fund.

Actually that is not the case. Donald F. Regan remarked recently that "In turn the United States is the second largest user of the entire membership. The U.S. drew upon IMF resources 18 times in the 1960s, six times in the 1970s, most recently in 1978, for a total of about $6.5 billion."[8]

As to the meaningfulness of the ratio as a creditworthiness indicator, the reader is referred to Table 4, which lists the Fund's holdings of a member's currency as percentage of the member's quota (a member's use of IMF funds).

The table clearly shows that as creditworthiness indicator, the Fund's holdings of a member's currency as percentage of the member's quota is practically meaningless, unless the holdings exceed 100 percent of the quota, meaning that the member is borrowing from the IMF. Members use their quotas on a routine basis.

RESERVES TO EXTERNAL DEBTS RATIO

Some analysts use the ratio Reserves To External Debts of a country. The usefulness of this ratio for creditworthiness analysis purposes is doubtful. Even disregarding the uncertainties surrounding the evaluation of official gold holdings (what will be the value of gold five or eight years hence?), one should keep in mind that the main purpose of the reserves is to help the country during emergencies and cyclical swings of its external revenues. The repayment of debts is only one of the purposes for which reserves could be used.

The ratio is unreliable for comparative purposes because it does not indicate when the debts become due. The amount of the reserves may be relevant for debts payable next year, but means little for debts payable 10 or 15 years hence.

[8]Donald F. Regan, The Wall Street Journal, February 8, 1983.

chapter 7

Other Variables: Debt Service Ratio, Inflation, and External Debt Profile

DEBT SERVICE RATIO

The controversy about the meaning of the debt service ratio has been going on for decades.

Avramovic summarized the situation in 1964:

> "The use of this concept has been criticised, even by those who have been using it, as an inadequate measure of debt servicing burden. And yet, the ratio has shown strange powers of survival. The reasons are many, but three stand out. First, it is a seemingly simple and easily understandable relation—debt service against exports. Secondly, it can be computed on a firm statistical basis—it does not require the use of national accounts, with all the guesses involved in their compilation. Thirdly, economic analysts who have been aware of the imperfections of the ratio have failed to suggest an alternative."[1]

More recently, in 1977, Robert Z. Aliber stated that ". . . traditional debt service ratios have minimal value in predicting when individual developing countries' borrowers will not be able to meet their payments on schedule. . . . Countries with apparently high debt service ratios are likely to be able

[1]Dragoslav Avramovic, et al. *Economic Growth and External Debt*. Published for the World Bank by the Johns Hopkins University Press, Baltimore, Maryland, 1964; Chapter 4, Debt Sevice Ratio, under, 1 Rationale, p. 38.

to make their debt service payments on schedule as long as they avoid bouts of sharp currency overvaluation."[2]

Yet, as the reader will notice from Chapter 9, STRUCTURED SYSTEMS' OUTLINES AND MODELS, the ratio appears frequently in creditworthiness analysis systems. Therefore, it is advisable to examine it closely.

One should first look at its substance. World Bank data, on which the ratio is commonly based, include only official and officially guaranteed debts. Efforts are being made to obtain statistics about private debt servicing, but the results have not been encouraging.

From the viewpoint of the private lender, the ratio is meaningless, or worse, misleading, unless private debts are included.

Conceptual Weaknesses

Other things being equal, it should be obvious that the probability of prompt repayment of the external obligations of a country is higher when the servicing of the external obligations takes a relatively smaller share of its external revenues; conversely, the probability of prompt repayment diminishes as the share of external revenues preempted for debt servicing increases. As a performance indicator, the ratio has however a fundamental weakness, which was pointed out by Avramovic: "The debt service ratio is a cash flow concept rather than a profitability or productivity concept."[3]

Another conceptual weakness of the ratio is that the numerator includes "apples and oranges." Debit interest is an expenditure, a net drain on the resources of a country. Amortization is a financial transaction: on one side the external assets of a country are reduced by the payment, while at the same time its external liabilities are reduced by the same amount.

There is still another conceptual weakness. If one decides that both expenditures and repayments of capital should be included in the numerator, because the distinction between the two categories is not relevant, then both external earnings and capital inflows should also be included in the denominator. It is conceptually erroneous to include financial transactions in the numerator and exclude them from the denominator. The more so because most countries have current account deficits, and, in fact, the foreign exchange for the amortization repayment does not come from external earnings—it comes from new borrowing. But new borrowing or equity capital inflows cannot be included in debt servicing schedules because they are unknown quantities.

[2]Robert Z. Aliber. "Financing and Risk in Developing Countries." In Proceedings of a Symposium on Developing Countries' Debt. Sponsored by the Import-Export Bank of the United States, August 1977; Chapter 7, Panel Discussion: Private Bank Lending and the Debt Situation of the Developing Countries, p. 64.
[3]Op. cit., Aramovic, et al., Chapter 4, Debt Service Ratio, under 3, Long-Run Relevance, p. 42.

Liquidity Crises

Some observers feel that the debt service ratio can be used as an indicator of the short-term liquidity situation of a country. The problem is that the two- or three-year time lag with which the information becomes available is too long to allow for the use of the ratio as a warning signal. By the time it becomes available, the ratio is largely redundant.

However, servicing schedules published by the World Bank may show bunching of maturities in years ahead. That frequently leads to liquidity crises and should be taken as a warning signal.

Technical Problems

Comparability of the debt service ratio is another problem. The following examples show that the debt service ratio means different things in different countries.

Example 1

	Country A	Country B
Amount of debt servicing due	20	40
Gross External Revenues (GER)	100	200
Interest due	15	10
Amortization due	5	30
	. . . .	. . . .
Debt service ratio	20%	20%
Debit interest as percentage of GER	15%	5%

Assuming that interest rates on the external debts of the two countries are approximately on the same level, one should conclude that the size of the external debts of Country A, in relation to its external earnings, would be about three times higher than the relative size of the external debts of Country B, although the two countries have identical debt service ratios.

Example 2

	Country A	Country B
Total External debt	1,000	400
Gross External Revenues (GER)	1,000	1,000
Interest due	100	40
Amortization due	100	160
	. . . .	. . . .
Debt service ratio	20%	20%

The debt service ratios are identical, although the external indebtedness (related to foreign exchange earnings) is two and one half times higher for Country A.

The debt service ratio is also a poor indicator of underlying trends; it has a tendency to be erratic. The bunching of maturities causes a deterioration of the ratio in some years and a subsequent improvement when loans are refinanced.

For instance, the "Service Payments on External Public Debts as Percentage of Exports of Goods and Services, 1970–76" tables[4] list the following ratios in the Latin American section:

	1973		1974		1975		1976
Argentina	17.8	down to	16.6	up to	21.4	down to	18.3
El Salvador	5.4	down to	4.9	up to	9.3	down to	4.2
Paraguay	10.3	down to	7.7	up to	9.8	down to	8.7
Venezuela	6.0	down to	4.2	up to	5.4	down to	3.9

Service Payments

It would seem that the credits were on a two-year renewal cycle. No conclusion as to the underlying trends can be drawn from the seesaw motion of the ratio.

It is obvious that the conceptual weaknesses and the practical inconsistencies of the debt service ratio are due to the inclusion of amortization in the numerator of the ratio.

How significant would be a ratio without amortization? The feasibility of using such a ratio for creditworthiness evaluation purposes is explored in Chapter 16, FINANCIAL INCOME AND EXPENDITURES.

INFLATION

Inflation Rates and Debt Reschedulings

On the basis of experience with developing countries' debt rescheduling during the period 1960 to 1976, Nicholas Sargen makes a strong case for the use of wholesale price index (WPI) or consumer price index (CPI) increases as indicators of a country's future external payment difficulties.[5]

Sargen stated in 1977 that major international banks by and large consider the probability of widespread defaults on developing country loans as being

[4]World Debt Tables. Volume I, External Public Debt of Developing Countries, Document of the World Bank, October 20, 1978, pp. 212–213.
[5]Nicholas Sargen. "Banking in the World Economy, Economic Indicators and Country Risk Appraisal," Economic Review, Federal Reserve Bank of San Francisco, Fall 1977, pp. 19–35.

remote. A more likely scenario is that individual countries occasionally may experience repayment difficulties requiring some refinancing or rescheduling. Most banks, therefore, believe that the crucial prooblem is to be able to detect in advance which countries are likely to experience repayment problems and when these difficulties may arise.

A sample of 44 countries—those selected had a debt-service ratio above 5 percent, and time series data were available back to 1960—shows that all six countries which had wholesale price index (WPI) increases above 20 percent had to reschedule at least once between 1960 and 1976; of eight countries with WPI increases between 10 and 20 percent, one half had to reschedule; of 26 countries with WPI increases below 10 percent, only four had to reschedule.

Sargen's study notes that three of the countries with WPI increases between 10 and 20 percent which avoided rescheduling had frequent exchange rate adjustments. That suggests that increased exchange rate flexibility may help mitigate the adverse effects of inflation on the external accounts.

The study addresses itself to the problem of distinguishing the characteristics of the countries that have rescheduled their debts from those which have not done so. Two sets of variables were used for that purpose.

The first set includes variables most commonly used for the debt service approach:

1. debt service ratio
2. reserves-import ratio
3. export growth rate (in U.S. dollars)
4. growth of real GNP
5. level of per capita GNP in U.S. dollars.

The second set includes variables suggested by the monetary approach:

6. inflation rate (consumer prices)
7. growth rate of M1 money supply
8. a measure of relative purchasing power parity (the difference between the domestic and U.S. inflation rates, on a wholesale price basis, less the rate of domestic currency depreciation vis-a-vis the U.S. dollar).

Sargen found that the reserves-import ratio and the level of per capita GNP add little in the way of explanatory power. On the other hand, inflation rates and debt service ratios were found to be significant indicators. The mean inflation rate for the rescheduling group was nearly seven times higher than that of the non-rescheduling group. The scheduled debt-service ratio was found to be an accurate, but because of the time lag, largely ineffective indicator of reschedulings associated with external payments crises.

Inflation as Creditworthiness Indicator

Since consumer price indexes (CPI) are available for a wide range of countries
with relatively short time-lags, one should examine their usefulness for creditworthiness evaluation purposes.

One should keep in mind, however, that the CPI does not reflect price
trends of internationally traded goods. In some instances such as petroleum or
copper, the relationship is remote. The CPI reflects essentially domestic conditions that may affect the external accounts of a country.

Whether one should use consumer price or wholesale price indexes is
debatable. In industrial countries wholesale prices are probably more closely

Table 5   Consumer Prices Index (CPI) Percentage Increases*

	Averages				Averages		
	78/80	79/80	1980		78/80	79/80	1980
Switzerland	2.8	3.7	3.7	Costa Rica	10.9	13.6	17.6
Germany	4.2	4.8	5.2	New Zealand	14.3	15.4	17.6
Austria	4.5	5.0	5.7	United Kingdom	13.3	15.9	18.1
Belgium	5.2	5.6	6.3	Ireland	13.0	15.8	18.4
Netherlands	4.9	5.6	6.3	Philippines	14.7	18.6	18.5
Malaysia	5.3	5.1	6.8	Indonesia	16.2	20.2	18.9
Japan	5.1	5.6	7.9	Syria	9.5	11.8	19.0
Tunisia	7.8	8.9	9.4	Thailand	12.5	14.7	19.5
Morocco	9.2	8.9	9.7	Egypt	13.9	15.2	20.4
Australia	9.1	9.3	10.0	Italy	15.9	18.0	21.0
Canada	9.4	9.8	10.1	Venezuela	13.7	17.1	21.4
Norway	7.8	7.5	10.4	Paraguay	20.4	25.4	22.2
Guatemala	9.9	11.3	10.7	Greece	18.7	21.8	24.7
Zambia	12.7	10.5	11.5	Sri Lanka	16.4	18.2	26.0
Pakistan	9.3	10.5	11.6	Mexico	20.8	22.4	26.6
Finland	9.0	9.6	12.1	Colombia	23.1	25.5	26.8
Ecuador	11.7	11.5	13.0	Jamaica	30.4	27.9	26.8
France	11.0	11.9	13.1	So. Korea	20.4	23.5	28.5
United States	10.7	12.4	13.3	Tanzania	18.6	22.0	30.5
Kenya	12.9	10.8	13.6	Chile	36.2	34.3	35.2
So. Africa	12.2	13.4	13.6	Bolivia	25.8	33.4	47.7
Cyprus	10.3	11.4	13.7	Iceland	48.5	50.7	55.8
Sweden	10.3	10.6	13.8	Brazil	58.1	67.8	82.9
Honduras	11.3	14.3	15.4	Turkey	73.2	78.7	94.1
Spain	17.0	15.3	15.6	Israel	86.6	104.7	130.9
Malta	9.2	11.5	16.1				

*In order of 1980 increase.
Source: *IFS*, December, 1981.

related to international prices than consumer prices. On the other hand, a reduction in wholesale prices may be caused by a slowdown in a country's economy rather than being due to a decrease of inflationary pressures.

As a practical matter, consumer prices are more widely reported than wholesale prices; their use offers a wider basis of comparison.

Table 5 reports the CPI increases of 51 countries for the periods 1978 to 80, 1979 to 80, and 1980. The countries are listed in the order of their 1980 CPI increase.

The table shows a poor inflation/creditworthiness correlation. The United States is in 19th place and to find countries such as Tunisia, Morocco, Guatemala, Zambia, Pakistan or Ecuador listed ahead of the U.S. generates considerable doubt about the advisability of using consumer price indexes for creditworthiness evaluation purposes.

On the other hand, changes in the relative purchasing power of a currency, not reflected by exchange rate adjustments, may cause considerable problems (see Chapter 12 under "Changes of a Currency's Relative Purchasing Power").

Money Supply

Changes in money supply are sometimes used as indicators of future accelerating inflation. Apart from the uncertainty about the money supply measure to be used—M1, M2, or M3—there is the uncertainty about inter-country comparability of money supply data.

One should also keep in mind that money velocity (GNP divided by money supply) may be as much as five times higher in one country than in another. Inter-country comparisons of changes in money supply are meaningless unless adjusted for money velocity.

In view of these uncertainties, it seems doubtful that money supply comparisons are of practical help in creditworthiness evaluations.

Government Deficits

Government deficits as percentage of GNP are also used by some analysts for creditworthiness evaluation. The assumption is that in most developing countries the government will have to take recourse either to the printing press or increase its external borrowing.

The problem with the ratio is lack of inter-country comparability. The size of the government deficit depends on the size of the government sector, on the extent of its centralization, and on the extent of its social programs. Inter-country comparisons are unreliable.

However, government deficit changes could be used as warning signals. If there is an unusual increase in the size of the deficit, one could assume that there will be external payment difficulties in the future.

EXTERNAL DEBT PROFILE

A debt profile of the borrower, indicating the total outstanding and maturities is, of course, very useful information for the creditworthiness evaluation.

The principal sources for data on external debts are:

— the International Monetary Fund (IMF).
— the World Bank
— the Organization for Economic Co-operation and Development (OECD)
— the Bank for International Settlements (BIS)
— Morgan Guaranty Trust Company
— Euromoney Publications, London
— reports of the central banks

The International Financial Statistics (IFS) of the IMF reports monthly country borrowings from the Fund.

The World Bank publishes *Borrowing in International Capital Markets* and *World Debt Tables* which report "External Public Debt and Publicly Guaranteed Debt, Which Has an Original or Extended Maturity of Over One Year." External debts of more than one hundred developing countries are reported, with subtotals for Government Lenders, International Organizations, Suppliers, Financial Lenders, and Other Private Lenders.

The Organization for Economic Co-operation and Development (OECD) recently published *External Debt of Developing Countries—1982 Survey.* The survey is based on:

— the OECD Creditor Reporting System
— the World Bank Debtor Reporting System
— other official sources
— OECD Secretariat estimates.

The Bank for International Settlements (BIS) publishes a quarterly report *International Banking Developments*, which shows, among other data, the total lent to various countries and their residents by banks in 15 reporting countries, and the deposits of each debtor country and its residents with banks in the reporting countries.[6]

The Morgan Guaranty Trust Company publishes a monthly *World Financial Markets* study with a "publicly announced Eurocurrency bank credits" table a "new international bond issues" table.

---

[6]Austria, Belgium, Canada, Luxembourg, Denmark, France, Germany, Ireland, Italy, Japan, Netherlands, Sweden, Switzerland, United Kingdom, and United States.

Euromoney Publications also publishes monthly tables of borrowing by country and by economic area (Centrally Planned, OEDC, and so on).

The information available is plentiful. The problem is that it is not homogeneous. Some sources classify loans on the basis of their original length, others on the basis of the remaining length; some data are based on debtors' reports, others on creditors' reports; the conversion of various currencies into a standard currency may be based on end of period exchange rates, or on average rates; some sources report credit commitments, others disbursements; some data are published monthly, others quarterly or annually; the time lag varies from a few months to a couple of years, and there are duplications and omissions.

Inevitably country external debt totals will have to be estimated. To check the reliability of the estimates, one should calculate the totals for a few years and compare them with the foreign exchange flows indicated in the balance of payments. By definition a deficit in current account—adjusted by changes in reserves—has to be financed by equity capital inflows or by borrowing abroad.

International Development Association (IDA) credits should be listed separately in the debt profile since they are granted with 50-year maturity, have a 10-year grace period, pay no debit interest, and are charged only an annual service fee of 0.75 percent on the amount disbursed.

chapter 8

General Considerations: Judgmental Evaluations, Overall Country Ratings, Internal Procedure, The Report, and Country Risk Insurance

JUDGMENTAL EVALUATIONS

The evaluation of a country's creditworthiness is inevitably a mixture of an analytical examination of factual data and subjective judgments about imponderable social and political factors.

There is almost no limit to the number of imponderable factors that could be included in the creditworthiness evaluation. The reader is referred to "Commonly Used Judgmental Evaluation Factors" in Chapter 9.

Great efforts have been made in the last decade or so to quantify social, political, and economic imponderables, but the fact remains that many factors cannot be measured. Numbers or letters attributed to imponderable factors express only the analyst's opinion, which may differ from other opinions. For instance, it is very unlikely that several independent analysts would give the same score to the monetary policies followed by a country's authorities.

At any rate, judgmental evaluations are frequently included in the final score assigned to a country. Sometimes the procedure followed to arrive at a score is highly structured. The *World Political Risk Forecasts* of Frost and Sullivan are an example.

Political Risk Forecasts

Frost & Sullivan Inc. publishes a monthly political risk appraisal service called *World Political Risk Forecasts* (WPRF) which is intended to help executives assess the probability that foreign investments may be adversely affected by political changes.[1]

The service, which covers more than 80 countries, consists of individual country reports, updates, and a monthly newsletter containing updates for countries in the news and a "Summary of Political Risk Scores" table.

The country report—approximately 50 pages of text—describes the basic political situation of each country. The report lists the "actors" in each country's political system, their political aims, and their ability to affect the political risk in the country.

The actors selected may be individuals, groups, or ministries within the government, opponents of the government, and individuals or groups in the society such as businesses, unions, or ethnic organizations. Actors may also include foreign individuals or institutions, such as the International Monetary Fund, or other governments.[2] At least seven actors are suggested.

The monthly newsletter indicates letter-ratings, ranging from A+ to D−, for the finance risk, the investment risk, and the exporting risk of each country for the next 18 months and the next five years. The letter-ratings are best viewed as concise summaries of each country report; they can be used for quick reference, and what is more important, for comparisons among the countries listed in the monthly newsletter.

The scores are based on the analyses and forecasts of 250 country specialists, who may be classified in four main categories: Academic Specialists (about 60 percent), Consultants (about 20 percent), Specialists with Government Background (about 15 percent), and Business Specialists (about 5 percent).[3]

The Chemical Bank uses a similar system for the political risk evaluation.[4]

Ratings Based on Evaluations of Leading International Banks

The Institutional Investor publishes twice a year (March and September) country credit ratings based on ratings provided by leading international banks.

"Bankers are asked to grade each of the countries on a scale of zero to 100, with zero representing the least creditworthy countries and 100 representing the most creditworthy and the ones with the least chance of default. The sample of the study, . . . ranges from 75 to 100 banks, each of which provides its own

[1]Frost & Sullivan, Inc. *World Political Risk Forecasts*. New York, N.Y.; User's Notes, 1984.
[2]Ibid.
[3]Ibid.
[4]Joseph J. Tunney. *Assessing Country Risk*. Euromoney Publications, London, 1981; Chapter 7, Bank Perspectives in Measuring Risk, pp. 83–85.

ratings. All participants in the survey are assured that their responses and the fact of their participation are kept strictly confidential. Banks are not permitted to rate their home countries. The individual responses are weighted, using an Institutional Investor formula that properly gives more weight to responses from banks with the largest worldwide exposure and the most sophisticated country analysis systems."[5]

Banks, of course, take such ratings into account in their creditworthiness evaluations. They are important because they indicate to what extent each country has (or does not have) access to commercial banking credit.

Market Determined Spread as Creditworthiness Indicator

The controversy about the superiority of market assessments over experts' evaluations extends also to the international creditworthiness field.

Monroe J. Haegele states "The premise behind traditional country risk analysis is that the analyst can arrive at a better judgment than the market has already made. The evidence we have assembled, though preliminary, would suggest that this premise is false."[6]

Past experience does not confirm the accuracy of market assessments. The optimistic market assessments of the 1920s about international bonds were disproven by the almost universal defaults of the 1930s. It is questionable whether recent market assessments are in any way superior to traditional country evaluations.

The "Country Risk League Table" for February 1982,[7] for instance, rates Greece and Indonesia ahead of Belgium, Denmark, Italy or Spain, while the Institutional Investor of March 1982 (based on ratings provided by leading international banks) ranks Belgium, Italy, Denmark and Spain ahead of Greece and Indonesia.

Nevertheless such ratings should be taken into account in the creditworthiness evaluation because they indicate a country's (changing) access to financial markets.

OVERALL COUNTRY RATINGS

To use, or not to use, overall country ratings is a difficult dilemma.

Some observers feel that to provide a country report with no bottom line, or specific conclusion readily understandable by bank officials, lessens the an-

---

[5]*The Institutional Investor*, New York, N.Y., March 1983, p. 60.
[6]Monroe J. Haegele. *Assessing Country Risk*. Euromoney Publications, London, 1981; Chapter 6, Using a Market Determined Spread as a Guide, p. 75.
[7]*Euromoney*. Euromoney Publications, London, February 1982, The Country Risk League Table, pp. 47–51.

alyst's effectiveness even though the overall analysis may be excellent. Inter-country comparisons are uncertain without specific ratings.

On the other hand, John A. Holsen states that " . . . our experience (is) that there is no adequate checklist or formula which takes into account all the relevant variables; such techniques can be no more than starting points for country evaluation."[8]

Roman Senkiw's negative opinion about overall ratings is even stronger. He states that "I would also offer the general remark that using checklists . . . is only better than nothing at all. The main problem is that checklists add apples and oranges and it is impossible to interpret the meaning of the final number that is derived. It may be of some value to have the person in charge of a country go through such an exercise, but it isn't useful to derive any overall scores by this method. This is, in fact, why the Royal Bank eliminated the checklist system several years ago."[9]

Weaknesses of Overall Country Ratings

In order to obtain overall country ratings, the analyst will have to solve two problems:

— the quantification of human factors, and
— the selection of credible weights for each factual variable and for each human factor.

As to human factors, the overall rating will have to take into consideration such political factors as the probability that war, riots, revolution, or other events that may unfavorably affect foreign creditors may occur. The probability that such events may happen must be evaluated and quantified by the analyst and then worked into the overall rating. However, at present there is no solid basis for a probability computation that any of these events may occur. The analyst's evaluation of the probabilities is only an educated guess, it is not the result of a probability computation. To include subjective judgments in the calculation of an overall rating conveys the impression of a scientific substance and precision that in fact do not exist.

Obvious examples are creditworthiness ratings given to South Korea or Taiwan. What are the probabilities that an armed conflict may start between North and South Korea? Or the probabilities that the People's Republic of China may try to invade Taiwan within a certain period of time, say within the next

---

[8]John A. Holsen. "Financing and Risk in Developing Countries." In *Proceedings of a Symposium on Developing Countries' Debt.* Sponsored by the Export-Import Bank of the United States, August 1977; Chapter 13, World Bank Techniques for Country Evaluation, p. 102.

[9]Op. cit., Roman Senkiw, Chapter 14, Panel Discussion: Managing and Assessing Developing Country Risk, p. 109.

five years? It would be unreasonable to answer such questions with a numerical expression of probabilities.

Emotional, and sometimes irrational, actions involved in political decisions which affect a country's repayment capability are unpredictable.

Working factual data into an overall score is not an unequivocal process either, since it requires the selection of weights to be attributed to each variable in the model. By selecting different weights one would obtain different scores.

Another problem is the selection of the length of time to be used for the evaluation of past performance. The lack of defaults in the 1920s was at that time considered significant for the evaluation of the risk involved in buying foreign bonds, an assumption shattered by the defaults of the 1930s. Similarly, the very few defaults of the post World War II period gave lenders a false sense of security.

Most banks are aware that mechanically calculated overall country ratings are of doubtful reliability; they solve the problem by using ratings based on a number of factual variables as a starting point and then use qualitative judgments to reach an overall evaluation.

INTERNAL PROCEDURE

There is a fair degree of similarity among the country evaluation procedures used by commercial banks. Differences are due mostly to the size of the international operations. In banks with extensive international operations and foreign branches, the process starts abroad and continues through various levels until it reaches the top. The procedure is intended to determine:

— the degree of risk involved in dealing with a country, and
— exposure limits as a function of
  — the size of a country's economy
  — the size of the overall commitment the bank wishes to make (in which the size of its capital is one of the factors).

A few typical examples are reported below.

Toronto Dominion Bank

Toward the end of the year, a schedule for country review is established for the coming year. The number of countries given full review is normally from 60 to 70. A further 20 to 30 countries are reviewed using a "short format."[10] The steps are:

[10]"Role of Department of Economic Research in Country Risk Assessment," The Toronto-Dominion Bank, Toronto, Ontario. Memorandum, December 1981.

1. A country review is completed in the Department of Economic Research (DER).
2. The Regional Division adds a summary of the bank's activity in the country concerned, plus an overall assessment which takes into account the DER report, marketing considerations, and anything else the Regional Division feels relevant.
3. The whole package is sent to the International Banking Group (IBG) Credit Department, which can endorse or amend the proposed lending limit.
4. The final stage is approval of the limit by a senior Head Office executive.

The procedure assigns a leading role to the Regional Division, which must ultimately take responsibility for loans.

Bankers Trust

The Bankers Trust procedure is a good example of the qualitative approach. Lawrence J. Brainard states that the bank's risk evaluation method " . . . reflects the conviction that country assessments must rest on the qualitative judgments of the bank's own professional economists and bankers. A variety of econometric models and ranking schemes were examined when the present country review system was set up. Such approaches inevitably involve qualitative judgments in scoring and entering quantitative data. It was felt that an effective country assessment system should aim at getting the various qualitative judgments onto the table for examination and discussion, rather than implicitly including such judgments in quantitative rankings."[11]

A country risk meeting is the key element in the Bankers Trust country assessment system. "Several days prior to the meeting, a country risk review is circulated to participants in the meeting. This review consists of two parts: the first is prepared by the bank's economic and political analysts, and the other by the lending officer for the country."[12] The reports are prepared according to a structured format.

The review prepared by economic and political analysts contains four brief one or two-paragraph summaries covering:

1. The domestic economy.
2. The foreign economy (trade and foreign debt position).

---

[11]Lawrence J. Brainard. *Assessing Country Risk.* Euromoney Publications, London, 1981; Chapter 9, Bankers Trust Approach to International Risk Assessment, p. 93.
[12]Ibid., p. 94.

3. The policy environment (the rationality of the country's social-economic goals and the efficiency of the policies used to attain these goals).
4. The political-social environment.

The independent assessment written by the lending officer addresses only the policy environment and the political-social environment.

Brainard adds "We do ask the economist and the lending officer to stick their necks out by providing an explicit statement of their assessments. . . . Rather than trying to reach a consensus, the discussion process seeks to explore the reasons why assessments may differ."[13]

THE REPORT

The report submitted to management is the end result of the whole creditworthiness evaluation process. It is what management will see and will have to act upon. Theoretically it may be advisable to submit a comprehensive report, a study in depth; but the time pressures of modern life require that the report should be as short as possible.

Thomas J. Reckford remarks "You can write a carefully phrased 30-page paper, and it will sit on someone's desk for months. A good executive summary is essential—a two-page summary—and will very often be the only part of your paper that anybody reads."[14]

Toronto Dominion Bank's normal country review runs to about 2,000–2,500 words of text, backed up by four tables. The text is customarily divided into four sections:

1. Summary and appraisal.
2. Developments in the domestic economy.
3. External section.
4. Prospects section (focuses on the longer term outlook).

The four tables are:

1. Summary of the other three tables.
2. Domestic economy.
3. Balance of payments.
4. External debt.

[13]Ibid., p. 94.
[14]Op. cit., Thomas Reckford, Chapter 18, Information: Collation and Assessment, p. 146.

A short format is occasionally used for developed countries where there has been no obvious change in the perceived risk, or for smaller countries where the bank has little or no exposure. The short format comprises about 500–1,000 words of text as well as one statistical table similar to the summary table in the normal format.

COUNTRY RISK INSURANCE

Some readers may be interested in the options open for insuring international risks.

Cecil Hunt lists some of the possibilities:[15]

— Export-Import Bank—U.S. contractor's guarantee program.
— Overseas Private Investment Corp. (OPIC), coverage for on-demand bid, performance, and advance payment guaranties.
— Foreign Credit Insurance Association (FCIA) for services (management consultants, engineering services, and transportation companies).
— Private political risk insurance, such as American International Group, INA, Lloyds of London, etc.

Insurance programs are generally aimed at assisting exports, construction contractors, and investments abroad. Premiums are too high for their use in international lending.

Banks have used OPIC guarantees for the insurance against political risks of capital or operating funds allocated to branches or subsidiaries in foreign countries.

Examples are:[16]

— Bank of America, for a total of	$ 2.2 million
— Chase Manhattan Bank	2.0 million
— Citibank N.A.	18.7 million
— First National Bank of Boston	2.5 million

---

[15]Op. cit., Cecil Hunt, Chapter 17, Insuring for Political Risk, pp. 137–142.
[16]1980 Annual Report. Overseas Private Investment Corporation, Washington, D. C., pp. 53–55.

chapter 9

Structured Systems' Outlines and Models

A number of structured systems' outlines and models used by banks and other entities are reported in this chapter.

International creditworthiness evaluation systems have changed over the years. To give an indication of the changes that took place, the review of systems used by private lenders starts with a pre-World War II evaluation outline. That is followed by a table showing five illustrative country risk model outlines which show recent changes in short and medium-term risk models.

Several banks are modifying their evaluation systems. One example is listed after the five illustrative models given in this chapter. Several outlines of bank systems are listed next, followed by models used by industry, consultants, and rating agencies.

No attempt is made to separate qualitative systems from quantitative systems since most banks combine the two methods.

Although the outlines mention names of banks or other entities, the reader should be aware that the outlines and opinions are those of the economists or executives who prepared the papers. That means that the system outlined is not necessarily the one used by the bank indicated or that the system has not been changed. The outlines are abstracted from memoranda, presentations or publications received; it is possible that some of the finer analytical points may have been overlooked in the summarization. Apologies are extended to the authors.

The structured outlines and models are followed by a list of most commonly used variables, derived from the outlines and models reported in the following pages and from information supplied by the following banks:

— Banca Nazionale del Lavoro
— Credito Italiano
— Girard Bank
— Midland Bank plc
— National Bank of Detroit
— National City Bank (Cleveland)
— Northern Trust Company
— Security Pacific National Bank.

INDICATIVE THRESHOLDS

One of the peculiarities emerging from a review of commonly used credit evaluation variables is that there is no generally accepted threshold for each variable dividing good risks from bad risks.

A few indicative thresholds mentioned in the reference material consulted, are listed below.

For the Debt Service Ratio, which is mentioned in most systems, only two indicative threshold references were found. Alexander McW. Wolfe, Jr. states "Generally, a debt service ratio below 10% is acceptable whereas a ratio above 20% is potentially dangerous.[1] David Kern states "When it (debt service ratio) increases above 20–25 percent, it usually indicates a significant burden."[2]

For the ratio Reserves to Imports Wolfe states "Reserves adequate to cover three months of imports is generally considered a 'safe' level."[3] Kern states "As a general rule, if reserves cover less than two months of an LDC's average imports, that country may be faced with growing short-term pressures."[4] The Royal Bank of Canada manual on country risk states that if only the central bank holds foreign exchange, or if the country does not have strict exchange controls, and the ratio of "reserves as percent of imports" drops below 10 percent, roughly below one-month import coverage, the country is running a tight liquidity position.[5]

Regarding the Net External Debt as Percentage of GDP, the Royal Bank of Canada country risk manual states "Net debt as percentage of GDP should

---

[1]Alexander McW Wolfe. "Offshore Lending by U.S. Commercial Banks. Bankers' Association for Foreign Trade, Washington, D.C., and Robert Morris Associates, Philadelphia, PA.; Chapter 2, International Lending Risks, Part I, Country Risk, under Selected Indicators of Economic Growth and Creditworthiness, p. 51.
[2]David Kern. "More Need Than Ever for Assessing Risk in Overseas Loans." The Bankers' Magazine, London, February 1982; p. 34.
[3]Alexander McW. Wolfe, op. cit., p. 35.
[4]David Kern, op. cit., p. 35.
[5]"Notes on the Country Risk Assessment Process," The Royal Bank of Canada, Montreal, July 1983, p. 10.

be considered reasonable if below 20 percent."[6] Kern states "A debt to GNP ratio in excess of 40 percent is usually a sign of long-term financial problems, but is not necessarily a sign of weakness."[7]

Concerning the <u>Net Debt as Percentage of Exports</u> ratio, the Royal Bank of Canada country risk manual states "it can be anywhere up to 100 percent."[8] The Morgan Guaranty Trust Company, on the other hand, states "The incidence of debt reschedulings has been considerably higher for countries with debt to exports ratios that exceed 160 percent. Virtually every country whose ratio climbed beyond 200 percent at one time or another has been forced to reschedule portions of its debt."[9]

Regarding the <u>Deficit of the Balance of Payments in Current Account as Percentage of GNP</u> ratio, Kern states "A sustained deficit in excess of $7\frac{1}{2}$ to 10 percent usually indicates deep-seated economic weaknesses."[10]

Concerning the <u>Short-Term Debt to Imports</u> ratio, Morgan Guaranty states "short-term debt generally should not exceed an amount equivalent to approximately three months of merchandise imports."[11]

OUTLINES OF STRUCTURED SYSTEMS AND MODELS

Various outlines of structured systems and models used by banks and other enterprises are listed in the following pages.

Outline 1

Pre World War II country risk evaluation criteria for international bond issues. *

These are some of the factors the bankers took into consideration:

1. The political situation:
   — prospects of peace or war,
   — stability of the foreign government,
   — relations between the United States and the debtor country, and so on.

---

[6]Ibid., p. 13.
[7]David Kern, op. cit., p. 35.
[8]The Royal Bank of Canada, op. cit., p. 13.
[9]World Financial Markets, June 1983, Morgan Guaranty Trust Company of New York, p. 4.
[10]David Kern, op. cit., p. 35.
[11]Morgan Guaranty Trust Company of New York, op. cit., p. 5.
*Abstracted from "Deterioration in the Quality of Foreign Bonds Issued in the United States, 1920–1930", Ilse Mintz, National Bureau of Economic Research, Inc., New York, N.Y., 1951, pp. 73–74.

2. Character of the borrowing nation:
    —   its willingness to make sacrifices in order to pay its debts. This is
        important because some nations take advantage of any pretext to
        avoid paying which, since it is not feasible to force payment of
        foreign debts, is as bad as incapacity to pay. Other nations, on
        the contrary, go to great lengths to pay their debts.
3. The general economic situation of the debtor country:
    This would involve a careful analysis of:
    —   its past debt record,
    —   its record of income and expenditures for a period of from 5 to
        10 years preceding the time at which the loan is being considered,
        and its budget for the succeeding year or two years,
    —   its import and export statistics for the past 5 or 10 years and an
        analysis of its 'invisible' trade, if any,
    —   its national debt both on a total and a per capita basis,
    —   its national wealth,
    —   its fiscal position as to its holdings of gold or the gold holdings of
        its central bank in relation to its outstanding currency,
    —   value of its actual or potential trade with the United States.

This point, the economic position of the nation, was usually deemed to be
the most important factor even when the loan was granted to a private enterprise.

Outline 2

Illustrative country risk models   —   five "possible models which may help the
reader to appreciate how the approach to country risk assessment has developed
over the past few years . . . starting from very simplified structures often used
in the early 1970s"* are reported on page 69.

Kern notes "experience shows that it is simply not practical to try and capture
the entire spectrum of possible variables in any model. A more sensible and
fruitful approach is to . . . focus attention on a small number of factors (say
between 5 and ten) which appear to be particularly relevant."†

*David Kern, Manager Economic Analysis, Statistics and International Sections, National West-
minster Bank, *Journal of the Institute of Bankers*, June 1981, p. 78.
†Ibid., p. 77.

Factors Accounting for Country Risk	Historical Development of Short/Medium-Term Risk Models				
	a	b	c	d	e
FINANCIAL VARIABLES					
Debt service ratio	25	25	20	20	20
Outstanding debt as % of GNP (or debt as % of exports)	—	—	5	10	10
Import coverage	25	25	20	15	10
Current account deficit as % GNP	—	—	—	5	10
POLITICAL AND STRUCTURAL FACTORS					
Commodity dependence	30	20	20	10	10
Energy vulnerability	—	—	5	10	10
Political/strategic factors	10	20	20	25	30
Sophistication of financial institutions	10	10	10	5	—
Total	100%	100%	100%	100%	100%

Outline 3

Example of recent model change—John K. Thompson, International Economist, Mellon Bank N.A., Pittsburgh, Pa.*

The outline does not necessarily reflect the bank's country evaluation system which may have been subsequently changed.

Variables used:

1981		1983	
LIQUIDITY			
Reserves to Imports	40	Reserves to Imports	40
Debt service to Exports	20	Debt service due in 1 year plus assets of foreign banks due in 1 year to Exports of goods and services	20
Large reserves losses	10	Decline of reserves of more than 30% (15%) in last 3 years	10

*Abstracted from *Assessing Country Risk*. Euromoney Publications, London, 1981; Chapter 5, An Index of Economic Risk, pp. 71–72, and correspondence with Mr. Thompson. (Mr. Thompson left the Mellon Bank during the second half of 1983 to join the Organization for Economic Cooperation and Development, Paris.)

Late payment experience	10	Late payments or arrears to any banks or suppliers	10
IMF credit to Quota	20	Use IMF credit to quota	20
	100		100

STRUCTURAL ANALYSIS

% change in consumer prices		Average consumer prices increase:	
1 year	5		
5 year average	5	4 years	5
last year to 5 year average	5	last year to 4 year average	5
1 year % change M1 to % change real GDP (5 years)	10	1 year % change M1 % change real GDP (5 years)	10
Change central bank financing of government to monetary base (recent year)	5	Change domestic credit Monetary base (base year)	10
Purchasing power parity	10	Purchasing Power parity	10
Growth of exports:		Country export growth (1 year)	10
most recent year	10	to world export growth (1 year)	10
four year average	10	Country export growth (4 years) to world export growth (4 years)	10
Exports to GDP (1 year)	10	Exports G. & S. to GDP	10
Debt to Exports (1 year)	15	Total debt to Exports G. & S.	15
Savings to GDP (4 years)	10	Savings to GDP (4 years)	10
Growth real per capita GDP (five year average)	5	Growth real per capita GDP (five year average)	5
	100		100

Thompson remarks that "Political and social variables are missing, not because such factors are unimportant but because they are not quantifiable and can be obtained only through detailed country analysis. Nor does the index contain any measure of human factors such as the quality of economic management or the authorities' commitment to maintain their creditworthiness."[*]

---

[*] *Assessing Country Risk,* p. 74.

Outline 4

Rein Bakhoven, Assistant Manager, Economic Research Department, Algemene Bank Nederland, Amsterdam*.

The outline summarizes papers prepared by Mr. Bakhoven; it does not necessarily reflect the bank's country evaluation system, which may have been subsequently changed.

The bank uses an "Early Warning Indicator" and a "Country Classification" system, reflecting a country's solvency.

Early Warning Indicator

Starting point is the traditional debt service ratio—debit interest and amortization as percentage of export earnings; however the ratio is expanded by including interest and amortization on short-term debt, using statistical data of the Bank for International Settlements (BIS).

Bakhoven adds that 32 to 50 percent is considered a grey area, 50 percent plus is the area where liquidity problems may occur. Of course, the liquidity analysis is only one element of the creditworthiness analysis; the other element is solvency analysis, leading to:

Country Classification,   based on the following factors:

Per capita GNP (US$; 1978 prices)	Maximum	15
Exports (US$ bln; 1978 prices)	Maximum	15
Debt to exports G. & S.	Maximum	6
Export diversification	Maximum	5
Technology and management	Maximum	6
Potential of raw materials	Maximum	4
Political environment—internal situation	Maximum	6
Political environment—external situation	Maximum	6
Development and/or innovation philosophy	+	4
Reschedulings (added recently)	Minimum	−2
Use of Fund credit (added recently)	Minimum	−3

The "no risk" group has a score of 52 or more, the "high-risk" has a score of less than 13.

Bakhoven remarks "within our bank there has this year been renewed interest in the qualitative approach to country risk."

*Abstracted from papers prepared for the ABECOR Information Session on Country Risk Analysis, Brussels, May 1982, revised December 1983. ABECOR is an association of: Algemene Bank Nederland, Banca Nazionale del Lavoro, Banque Bruxelles Lambert, Banque Nationale de Paris, Barclays Bank, Bayerische Hypotheken-und Wechsel-Bank, Dresdner Bank AG., Oesterreichische Laenderbank, and Banque Internationale a Luxembourg.

Outline 5

Richard O'Brien, et al., Economics Unit, American Express International Banking Corporation, London*.

The outline summarizes the memorandum prepared by the Economics Unit; it does not necessarily reflect the bank's country evaluation system, which may have been subsequently changed.

Country Scoring System

1—Extent of foreign capital dependence	Score	15
2—Import dependence	Score	10
3—Vulnerability of revenues	Score	15
4—Debt servicing burden	Score	15
5—Monetary and fiscal control	Score	15
6—Hospitality to private and foreign capital	Score	5
7—Comparative importance of country	Score	5
8—Political risk	Score	20
	Total	100

The following details illustrate the way in which each question is answered:

1. Foreign capital dependence:
    1.1 The foreign savings gap
    1.2 External public debt as percent of current account receipts
    1.3 GDP per capita
    1.4 Current account gap as percent of current account receipts
    1.5 Current account gap as percent of GDP
3. Vulnerability of export revenues:
    3.1 Three commodities as percent of total
    3.2 One commodity as percent of export revenues
    3.3 Export growth rate

The final rating is a qualitative decision based on careful interpretation of the economic data and an assessment of the political situation in each country.

*Abstracted from memorandum "Country Risk Analysis Approach" May 1982.

Moreover, the rating can be changed if the credit assessor feels there are sufficient grounds for assessing the risk as being different from the statistically indicated rating. Each country is then assigned a basic rating ranging from A to E.

An asterisk warning signal system complements the system (from one to three asterisks depending on the seriousness of the warning).

Outline 6

Pier Luigi Gilibert, Banca Commerciale Italiana, Milan*.

The outline summarizes the memorandum prepared by Mr. Gilibert; it contains the Banca Commerciale Italiana model for country risk evaluation developed by the author.

Table 1—Macroeconomic variables (4 years)

— Budget deficit (% GDP)
— Money supply change (%)
— Increase consumer prices index (%)
— Increase GDP in real terms (%)
— Index export prices to import prices
— Country's export prices to competitors' export prices

Table 2—Balance of Payments (3 years)

Imbalance current account
  — goods
  — services
  — unrequited transfers
Imbalance capital account
  — direct investments
  — portfolio investments
  — short-term capital
  — long-term capital
  — net errors & omissions
Imbalance current account (% GDP)

Exports plus imports (% GDP)

*Abstracted from memorandum "Proposta di Analisi del Rischio Paese" (Proposed Country Risk Analysis System), October 1982.

Table 3—Reserves (3 years)

— Reserves minus gold
  — foreign exchange
  — SDRs
  — reserve position in Fund
— Gold (national valuation)
— Monetary authorities' short-term liabilities
— Net official reserves
— Monetary authorities' medium and long-term net position
Net official reserves as month-of-imports

Table 4—Short, medium and long-term external debt (3 years)

— Medium and long-term
  — due to official lenders (excluding IMF)
  — due to private lenders
— Due to IMF
— Short-term (due to banks reporting to BIS)
— Total
Short-term debt percent of net official reserves (see Table 3)

Short-term debt percent of total debt

Table 5—Debt service (projected for 5 years ahead)

1. Total debt service
    — principal payments
    — interest payments
    — due to private lenders
    — due to official lenders
2. Debt service percent of exports G&S
3. Debt service percent of GDP.

Table 6—Source of medium and long-term funds (last 3 years)

— Syndicated credits
— Foreign bonds
— Eurobands

The tables are accompanied by a report on the economic structure of the country, the social situation, political developments and its financial reliability.

Gilibert remarks that a country should not be examined as a separate case, but on a comparative basis, as part of a group of countries.

Outline 7

H. Robert Heller, Vice President for International Economics, Bank of America NT & SA, San Francisco*.

The outline is abstracted from Mr. Heller's presentation; it does not necessarily reflect the bank's country evaluation system, which may have been subsequently changed.

The country risk program utilizes a three-pronged evaluation system.

1. *Debt Service Capacity Index*
   a. external liquidity situation
   b. fiscal and monetary policies
   c. economic structure

   It was found that:
   a. liquidity factors are particularly relevant over the short-term (one year)
   b. a., b., and c. make up the medium-term index (3 years), which was chosen as basic indicator of a country's debt service capacity
   c. structural factors tend to dominate in the long-run (5 years).

2. *Judgmental Economic Indicator* (rating from A to F, based on a flexible questionnaire)

   Subjects covered:
   — effectiveness of monetary policy
   — government's fiscal policy
   — regulatory policies in the financial sector
   — government's attitude toward domestic and foreign investments
   — quality of management
   — economic structure (natural resources, labor force, infrastructures, composition total output)
   — export and import diversification
   — access to international credit
   — exchange rate policy

*Abstracted from "International Lending, Risk and Portfolio Quality", presentation at "Conference on the Conditions for International Monetary Stability", Montevideo, December 1981.

3. *Judgmental Political Indicator* covers three general areas:
a. Government control
—   government's effectiveness in formulating a coherent policy regarding important political and social problems
—   institutions designed to provide for a resolution of political and social conflict
—   orderly succession of government
—   institutional structures designed to bring competing influences to bear upon government policy.
b. Potential for social unrest
    —   as it might influence a country's debt service ability.
c. External factors
    —   potential security threats
    —   special relations with the United States
    —   relevant regional alliances.

The debt service capacity model is akin to a set of leading economic indicators and focuses on a country's ability to avoid arrears, reschedulings, and actual default on its foreign debt.

Outline 8

Banque PARIBAS, Paris*.
The outline is abstracted from the memorandum; it does not necessarily reflect the bank's country evaluation system, which may have been changed.

The bank uses a computerized data bank with a set of 40 economic indicators for each country.

Structural Analysis

1. International trade analysis
    —   commodity price trend
    —   international trade development prospects by product
    —   geographic and product dependence of the country
2. Geopolitical analysis
    —   world political zone
    —   lines of fracture which may become destabilization targets

*Abstracted from memorandum "Description and Method of Country Risk Evaluation", October 1982.

    — political and military dependences

    — monetary exchange zones

    — domestic destabilizing components (ethnic groups, social groups, army)

3. International capital market performance

    — foreign debt structure in terms of creditors

    — conditions of access to capital market: spread, terms and fees

    — country's image on the capital market as determined in cooperation with Paribas' financial operations division

4. Development prospects

    — mineral, agricultural and industrial wealth

    — choice of development model (growth by import substitution, tendency toward self-sufficiency, export led growth, etc.)

    — foreign financing, domestic resources and foreign exchange income prospects

    — adjustment capacity (flexibility of imports and exports in terms of GDP)

    — national savings to foreign debt flow ratio

Quantitative Analysis

— GNP

— Size of foreign debt

— Debt servicing and repayment schedule

— Estimated short-term debts and working capital

— Current foreign exchange income

— Current account balance

— Exchange reserves

— Inflation and exchange rate

— Budget deficit

Ratios

— External debt to GNP

— Debt servicing to current foreign exchange income

— International reserves in months-of-imports

A medium-term (up to 3 years) estimate of the country's foreign income and financial requirements (development plan, budget, debt servicing, foreign deficit) is then prepared.

In addition Parisbas relies heavily on information obtained from its foreign offices, monthly meetings of the French Banking Association, and other organizations in France and abroad.

Outline 9

Manfred Kraffczyk, Director Commerzbank, A.G., Duesseldorf*.
    The outline summarizes Mr. Kraffczyk's presentation; it does not necessarily reflect the bank's country evaluation system, which may have been subsequently changed.

The overall rating involves the assessment of three subordinate categories.

Economy

- gainful employment ratio
- economic growth in real terms
- inflation rate
- per capita GDP
- literacy rate
- raw material resources
- primary energy reserves
- foreign exchange reserves
- capacity to earn foreign exchange
- foreign indebtedness
- goods and service exports as percent of goods and service imports
- current account imbalance as percent GDP
- steadiness of export earnings and diversification of exports
- reserves as months-of-imports (good and services)
- foreign indebtedness as percent of GDP
- debt service ratio

Administrative Capacity

- based on answers to a list of about 50 questions to be answered "substantial," "average," or "low".

Political Stability

- political opposition
- political freedom
- ethnic minorities

*Abstracted from presentation in Waco, Texas, November 1980.

— distribution of income and wealth

— probability of war, political upheaval, and so on.

Different weight is given to each of the three categories depending on whether a country is industrialized, newly industrialized (NICs), less developed (LDCs), or least developed (LLDCs). Total zero to one hundred. Economy receives 55 percent of weight in all categories.

Outline 10

James A. Merrill, Senior Vice President and Chief International Economist, Marine Midland Bank, New York*.

The outline summarizes Mr. Merrill's presentation; it does not necessarily reflect the bank's evaluation system, which may have been subsequently changed.

The evaluation is based on the following elements:

Econometrics

— long-run indicators
    — debt service burden
    — level per capita income
    — level domestic credit creation
— short-run indicators
    — net foreign assets
    — gross reserve cover
    — trade account improvement or deterioration
    — domestic credit creation.

Country Risk Questionnaire   51 questions concerning

— domestic and international economics
— social and political factors.
    Every question must be answered on a scale from one to seven and has a predetermined weight; example:
— average rate export growth (10 years)
— product diversification
— value added in production

*Abstracted from "The Evaluation of Risk on a Geographical Basis", presentation at the IVth International Banking Seminar of the International Chamber of Commerce, Cannes, October 1980.

— oil imports
— level of debt and debt service;
— social and political factors consist of 13 questions and receive 40 percent of the total score.

Country Studies

— prepared at least annually for all countries rated A or B, and at least semi-annually for all countries rates C, D or E;
— prepared by regional economists to summarize analyses of short- and medium-term creditworthiness, including tables of data projecting balance of payments and external debt indicators.

Outline 11

A. Bruce Brackenridge, Executive Vice President Morgan Guaranty Trust Company, New York*.

The outline summarizes Mr. Brackenridge's presentation, it does not necessarily reflect the bank's country evaluation system, which may have been subsequently changed.

Country creditworthiness evaluation concentrates on four areas:

1. *Policy factor* — Emphasis is placed on the quality of a country's economic and financial management and whether the economic team is able to make its counsel felt among the country's political leadership. The promptness of current account adjustments in response to higher oil prices and world recession is considered a good test of the quality of economic teams throughout the world.
2. *Basic economic factors*
    a. Natural resources and potential for their development.
    b. State of human resources, for instance, the success with which the labor force can be educated and trained for increasingly complicated tasks; moreover, the entrepreneurial ability of the business group.
    c. The growth strategy followed in years past and at present should be in accord with the country's natural and human resources.
    d. It is important that a developing country be able to finance a significant portion of its investment requirements internally.

*Abstracted from "Financing and Risk in Developing Countries, *Proceedings of a Symposium on Developing Countries' Debt*, Sponsored by the Export-Import Bank of the United States" August 1977, pp. 72–75.

3. *External finance*
   a. The balance of payments outlook should be assessed in detail, with view of each of the important trends.
   b. Rate at which the country's external debt has been growing and its terms—burden of debt service on the balance of payments.
   c. Adequacy of official reserves, months-of-imports coverage.
4. *Political factors* — In assessing political stability one should look for reasonable assurance that, if political change comes, it will be orderly and there will be reasonable continuity in fundamental economic policies. In addition, a country's economic viability must be appraised in the context of the regional and worldwide political situation.

Outline 12

The Royal Bank of Canada, Montreal*.

The outline summarizes the Economics Department notes; it does not necessarily reflect the bank's country evaluation process, which may have been subsequently changed.

The system consists of three sections:

— Economic risk assessment
— Political risk assessment
— Business risk assessment

Economic Risk Assessment

The bank uses a two-tier approach:

— Early warning model
— Judgmental assessment

Early Warning Model

1. Trend in external sector's strength
   — export growth
   — trade balance

*Abstracted from "Notes on the Country Risk Assessment Process," Economics Department, July 1982.

— growth in reserves
— reserves over imports
2. International price competitiveness
— exchange rate
— domestic price performance relative to world developments
3. External public borrowing
— availability of IMF credit
4. Economic structure (judgmental)
— degree of development and diversification of the economy, exports
— export or import vulnerability
5. Access to capital markets (judgmental)
— country's ability to raise funds abroad

Judgmental Assessment (economic)

1. Domestic economy
— real economic growth
— inflation outlook
— monetary policy
— fiscal policy
2. External sector
— commodity price trends
— trend in export market share
— balance of payments outlook
3. Foreign debt
— relative size and growth of foreign debt
— debt service ratio
— debt rollover/cash flow

Politial Risk Assessment

— Political stability (succession process)
— External/internal relations
— Nationalization/expropriation record
— Attitude to foreign investments
— Quality of government administration

Business Risk Assessment

— Local financial markets and banking system
— Bankruptcy rate

— Country repayment record
— Quality of management
— Foreign exchange control

Numerical score in overall rating:
— Economic risk   300 points
— Political risk   200 points
— Business risk   100 points

The overall country risk rating is subject to review by the Country Review Committee (Divisional).

Outline 13

Alexander McW. Wolfe, Jr., Vice Chairman of the Board, Southeast Bank, N.A., Miami*.
The outline is abstracted from Mr. McW. Wolfe's paper, it does not necessarily reflect the bank's country evaluation system, which may have been subsequently changed.

Selected Indicators of Economic Growth and Creditworthiness.

Dynamic Indicators (at least five years)

— Growth in real GNP per capita
— Export growth
— Share of manufactured goods in total exports (over time)
— Debt service ratio
— Ratio of reserves to imports
— Rate of inflation

Level of Development Indicators

— GNP per capita
— GNP
— Agriculture to GNP

---

* Abstracted from "Offshore Lending by U.S. Commercial Banks." Bankers' Association for Foreign Trade, Washington, D.C., and Robert Morris Associates, Philadelphia, Pa., 1981; Chapter 2, International Lending Risks, Part I: Country Risk, pp. 43–61.

— Domestic investment to GNP
— Domestic savings to GNP

Ranking System   For each indicator each country is ranked, based on the value of the indicator, with a number from 1 to n (the total number of countries). The rank values for each variable are then combined in a total score. "Obviously, this system of empirical comparisons of countries cannot provide the last word in discussions and loan decisions about a country. Any analysis must include in-depth study of debt structure and judgments about the political climate. . . . The purpose of the country ranking system is to provide the first cut in planning a multi-country international strategy."*

Outline 14

Gordon Rayfield, Political Analyst, International Economics Group, General Motors Corporation, Detroit, Mi. †.

The outline is abstracted from Mr. Rayfield's paper, it does not necessarily reflect the corporation's country evaluation system, which may have been subsequently changed.

Economic Analysis

— structure of the country's economy
— stage of economic development
— level of industrialization and infrastructure
— growth rate
— inflation rate
— key economic actors (individuals, organizations, and/or institutions who determine the nature of economic planning, development and management).

Political Factors

— structure of politics and its stage of development
— constellations of power in society
— mechanism of control (corruption, repression, involvement of opposition groups)

---

*Ibid., p. 61.
†Abstracted from *Assessing Country Risk*. Euromoney Publications, London, 1981; Chapter 15, General Motor's Approach to Country Risk, pp. 129–133.

— system's mechanism of legitimation (democratic processes, party politics, religious, or nationalist movements)
— key political actors (government decision makers, technocrats and administrators, political parties, the military, the local business elite, unions, potential opposition groups, newspapers).

The purpose of the analysis is to determine whether a G.M. activity will be profitable, and whether that profit can be repatriated to the U.S., in U.S. dollars.

Outline 15

Stephen H. Goodman, Assistant Treasurer, International and Planning, Singer Company, Stamford, Conn.*.

The outline is abstracted from Mr. Goodman's paper, it does not necessarily reflect the company's evaluation system, which may have been subsequently changed.

Singer uses a qualitative approach to country risk evaluation. It also uses an early warning quantitative model.

Early Warning Indicators

1. ratio of disbursed debt outstanding to exports
2. ratio of international reserves to imports
3. ratio of imports to GDP
4. ratio of the reserve position in the fund (IMF) to imports
5. ratio of gross fixed capital formation to GDP
6. percentage change in the consumer price index.

The results of the early warning model are then combined with the results of the qualitative evaluations made by the operating division. From this combined approach, countries are grouped into four categories: high risk, moderate risk, low risk, and uncertain, where the two evaluations are different. Further analysis is devoted to countries in the "uncertain" group.

Singer is not concerned that the country will not pay its debts. Its only concern is that the company may not be able to earn and remit to headquarters a sufficient profit to justify either an investment or an on-going operation.

*Abstracted from *Assessing Country Risk*, Euromoney Publications, London, 1981; Chapter 12, Corporate Attitudes, pp. 111–115.

Outline 16

Business International Corp., New York, N.Y. *

Takes into consideration

— Risk (28 factors)
— Opportunity (15 factors)
— Operating conditions (13 factors)

Risk Factors

— Political change—institutional
— Political stability—social
— Attitude major opposition groups
— Probability opposition group takeover
— State role in economy
— Expropriation
— Limits on foreign ownership
— Restrictions on imports
— Privileged environment for local competition
— Export requirements
— Stability of labor
— Relationship with west
— Relationship with neighboring countries
— Terrorism
— Implementation of government policy
— Balance of payments
— Reserves/imports ratio
— Export composition
— Energy vulnerability
— Strength of economy
— Distribution of wealth
— Strength of currency
— Convertibility to foreign currencies
— External debt
— Profit repatriation controls

*Abstracted from "Country Assessment Service—Country Ratings" published by Business International Corp.

— Price controls
— Availability and cost of local capital
— Inflation level

Opportunity Factors

— Desire for foreign investment
— Attitude toward private sector
— Size/influence middle class
— Market size/GDP
— Real GDP growth rate
— Market wealth/GDP per capita
— Real growth of GDP per capita
— Industrialization
— BI/data market intensity indicator
— BI/data market size indicator
— BI/data market growth indicator
— Level of foreign direct investment
— Growth of foreign direct investment
— Fixed capital formation
— Foreign investment profitability

Operating Conditions

— Legal system, judiciary
— Bureaucracy and red tape
— Quality of infrastructure
— Limits to new investments
— Local content requirement
— Cultural interaction
— Corruption
— Expatriate environment
— Labor productivity
— Cost of local labor
— Availability of local labor
— Inflation environment
— Level of corporate taxation

Overall country risk ratings and overall country financial ratings are assigned to each country for each one of the next five years.

Outline 17

Frost & Sullivan, Inc., New York, N.Y.

The following outline listing variables included in the calculation of "World Political Risk Forecasts" is abstracted from the "User's Notes" of Frost & Sullivan.

The 18 month and five year World Political Risk Forecasts take into consideration the probability and risk of:

— regime changes
— political turmoil
— restrictions on international business
— restrictions on trade

The Prince Model* is the basis of the system. The experts indicate their estimates of the position of each "actor" (see Chapter 8, under "Political Risk Forecasts"), according to the following characteristics:

1. *Orientation*—the current general attitude of the actor toward the event or action, classified as: support, neutrality or opposition,
2. *Certainty*—the firmness of the actor's disposition classified as: extremely high, high, moderate, slight, or little/none,
3. *Power*—the degree to which the actor can influence the event or action, classified as in item 2,
4. *Salience*—the importance the actor attaches to supporting or opposing the event or action, classified as in item 2.

The charts obtained from the experts are analyzed and combined in a set of estimates.

The results are summarized under three headings: Finance Risk, Investment Risk, and Exporting Risk.

The variables used for *18 month forecasts* are:

Finance Risk: Restrictions on International Business (Prince probability), Exchange Controls, Payment Difficulties, Fiscal/Monetary Expansion, and International Expansion.

Investment Risk: Political Turmoil (Prince probability), Restrictions on International Business (Prince probability), Equity Restrictions, Local Partici-

---

*The Prince Model, developed by William D. Coplin and Michael K. O'Leary, is described in Everyman's PRINCE: A guide to understanding your political problems, (Duxbury Publishing Co., 1976).

pation, Taxation Discrimination, Repatriation Restrictions, Exchange Controls, and Labor Costs Expansion.

Exporting Risk Political Turmoil (Prince probability), Restrictions on International Business (Prince probability), Restrictions on Trade (Prince probability), Exchange Controls, Tariffs, Non-Tariff Barriers, Payment Difficulties, and International Expansion.

The variables used for *five year forecasts* of

Finance Risk, Investment Risk and *Exporting Risk* are: Political Turmoil, Restrictions on International Business, Trade Restrictions, Domestic Economic Performance, and International Financial Status.

Outline 18

Standard & Poor's Corporation, New York, N.Y.*

Rating Methodology Profile for Sovereign Governments

Political Risk

— Characteristics of political system
  A   Type of government
  B   Process and frequency of political succession
  C   Degree of public participation
  D   Degree of centralization in decision-making process
— Executive leadership
  A   Relationship with supporting government institutions
  B   Relationship with supporting political coalitions
— Government institutions
  A   Responsiveness and access to executive leadership
  B   Effectiveness and efficiency
  C   Policy responsibilities
— Social coalitions
  A   Major socio-economic and cultural groups (church, military, land-owners, management, labor, ethnic groups, and so on)
  B   Political parties and their constituencies
— Social indicators
  A   Level and growth of per capita income, and other measures of the standard of living

*Abstracted from Credit Overview International, 1983, pp. 30–31.

    B   Distribution of wealth and income
    C   Regional disparities
    D   Homogeneity of the populace
— External relations
    A   Relations with major trading partners
    B   Relationship with neighboring countries
    C   Participation in international organizations

Economic Risk

— Demographic characteristics
    A   Level and growth of population
    B   Age distribution
    C   Urbanization trends
— Structure of the economy
    A   Extent and quality of infrastructure
    B   Natural resource endowment
    C   Distribution of productive activities
    D   Public sector participation in productive activities
— Recent economic trends
    A   Composition and growth of aggregate demand (nominal & real)
    B   Domestic economy
    C   External sector
— Economic policy
    A   Price and wage policies
    B   Monetary policy
    C   Fiscal policy
    D   External policies

COMMONLY USED QUANTITATIVE VARIABLES AND RATIOS

Macroeconomic

— GDP growth (nominal and in real terms)
— Per capita GDP level
— Per capita GDP increase (real terms)
— Savings to GDP (over time)
— Investments to GDP (over time)

— Share foreign trade in GDP
— Current account deficit to GDP (over time)
— Debt service to GDP
— Debt service to savings
— Debt service to public revenues
— Debit interest and direct investments earnings of foreigners to GDP
— Short term external debt to GDP
— Foreign debt to GDP
— External liabilities (debt and equity) to GDP

— Consumer prices index CPI (over time)
— Wholesale prices index WPI (over time)
— Comparison CPI and WPI present rate with past rates
— Money supply growth
— Money supply growth to GDP growth
— Domestic assets banking system (over time)
— Domestic credit creation (over time)
— Currency to total bank deposits
— Government spending to GDP
— Tax revenues to GDP
— Government deficit to GDP
— Military spending to GDP
— Level of short-term and long-term interest rates (over time)
— Relative purchasing power of currency (inflation rate to exchange rate changes)

External Accounts

— Total reserves
— Total reserves changes over time
— Reserves minus gold
— Reserves minus gold over time
— Availability IMF credit
— IMF credit to gross reserves
— Net foreign assets
— External assets commercial banks
— Reserves to imports
— Months-of-imports covered by reserves

— External debt to reserves
— Short-term external debt to reserves

— Debt service ratio (and over time)
— Public debt to exports (goods and services)
— External debt to GDP
— Interest payments to exports (G & S)
— Current investment service ratio (includes debt service and profits on foreign owned investments)
— Principal payments to total external debt

— Total foreign debt
— Debt growth (%)
— External debt to current account receipts
— Composition external debt
— Debt to Western banks
— Time profile ratios
— Share short-term debt in total
— Borrowing on international markets
— Eurocurrency loans and bonds
— Average spread Euromarket borrowing

— Current account
— Current account imbalance over time
— Current account imbalance to exports (G & S)
— Current account to GDP
— Overall balance of payments over time
— Basic balance of payments over time
— Trade balance
— Trade balance over time
— Exports (goods)
— Export trends over time
— Export concentration
— Export concentration, excluding oil
— Export vulnerability
— Export stability
— Export diversity
— Export market concentration

— Exports goods and services
— Imports (goods)
— Import trends over time
— Import composition
— Import compressibility
— Import dependence
— Petroleum imports
— Trade account improvement/deterioration
— Terms of trade over time
— Main trading partners
— Percentage change exports to percentage change imports
— Import coverage (imports to exports)

Other Variables

— Major natural resources
— Population growth
— Population density
— Degree of literacy of people
— Per capita expenditure on education
— Percentage of university graduates in population
— Density of medical facilities
— Gainful employment ratio
— Employment by economic sector
— Unemployment trend
— Degree of union organization
— Consumption (individual households)
— Extent industrialization
— Import substitution industries
— Membership in trade pacts
— Membership in political and economic power blocks
— Bankruptcy rate

COMMONLY USED JUDGMENTAL EVALUATION FACTORS

— Type of government
— Orderliness of political succession
— Political stability

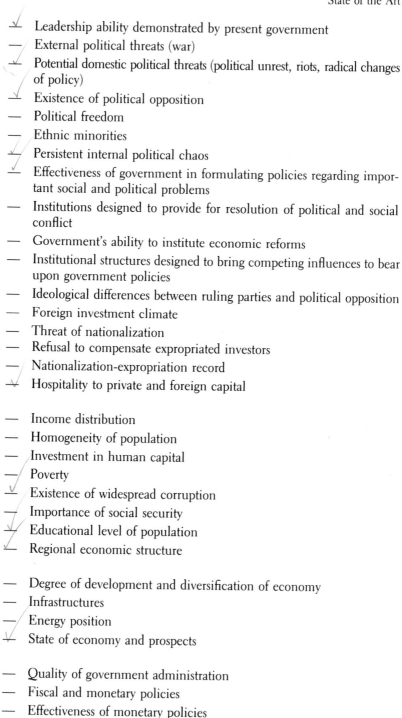

- Leadership ability demonstrated by present government
- External political threats (war)
- Potential domestic political threats (political unrest, riots, radical changes of policy)
- Existence of political opposition
- Political freedom
- Ethnic minorities
- Persistent internal political chaos
- Effectiveness of government in formulating policies regarding important social and political problems
- Institutions designed to provide for resolution of political and social conflict
- Government's ability to institute economic reforms
- Institutional structures designed to bring competing influences to bear upon government policies
- Ideological differences between ruling parties and political opposition
- Foreign investment climate
- Threat of nationalization
- Refusal to compensate expropriated investors
- Nationalization-expropriation record
- Hospitality to private and foreign capital

- Income distribution
- Homogeneity of population
- Investment in human capital
- Poverty
- Existence of widespread corruption
- Importance of social security
- Educational level of population
- Regional economic structure

- Degree of development and diversification of economy
- Infrastructures
- Energy position
- State of economy and prospects

- Quality of government administration
- Fiscal and monetary policies
- Effectiveness of monetary policies

— Government's economic development plans
— Current account adjustment policies
— Persistent overspending in public sector
— Wage-price policies
— Exchange rate policy
— Import restraint policy
— Control of inflation
— Foreign exchange controls
— Regulatory policies in financial sector

— Banking system
— Domestic capital markets
— Sophistication financial institutions
— Relative importance of private investments
— Access to foreign capital markets
— Reputation for economic stability
— Country's repayment record
— Current collection experience

— Quality of management in public and private sector
— Availability of technical and managerial skill
— Effectiveness of entrepreneurial class
— Labor force
— Ability to take part in complex modern occupations
— Unemployment as percent of labor force

— External debt under control
— Quality relationship with major trading partners
— Quality relationship with U.S.A.
— Quality relationship with IMF
— Willingness to provide data

III

Suggested Evaluation Procedure

chapter 10

Cost Effectiveness

Cost effectiveness should be taken into consideration when deciding upon country creditworthiness evaluation procedures.

The first step is to find out where the lending market is.

GROSS EXTERNAL REVENUES (GER)

Foreign exchange earnings indicate the size of a country's international trade, which generates international banking business and lending. A country with relatively modest foreign exchange earnings generates relatively modest international banking business and, what is worse, has relatively little foreign exchange to repay external obligations.

To spend money and time to analyze marginal, or not creditworthy countries, makes little sense. Therefore, the second step is to draw some kind of cost-effectiveness line for country evaluation expenditures.

Stephen H. Goodman distinguishes between " . . . the aid developing countries—where foreign exchange needs can be satisfied through grants or very soft loans—and the commercial developing countries who have regular access to, and rely on, commercial financing to cover their exchange requirements."[1] Aid developing countries are those in which commercial banks would be less interested.

WORLD BANK CLASSIFICATION

The above concept can be expanded by using information appearing in the *Annual Report* of the World Bank.

The World Bank is a group of three institutions, the International Bank for Reconstructions and Development (IBRD), the International Development Association (IDA), and the International Finance Corporation (IFC).

The common objective of these institutions is to help developing countries attain a higher level in standards of living by channeling financial resources from developed countries to the developing world.

IBRD loans are generally directed toward developing countries at more advanced stages of economic and social growth. Generally, such loans have a grace period of five years and are repayable over 20 years. The interest rate charged on the loans is calculated in accordance with guidelines related to the cost of borrowing. IBRD must pay due regard to the prospects of repayment.

IDA assistance is principally directed toward poorer developing countries, those with an annual per capita gross national product of less than $681 at 1979 prices.[2] The terms of IDA credits are: 10-year grace period, 50-year maturities and no interest. An annual service fee of 0.75 percent is charged on the disbursed portion of each credit.

IBRD loans are made to governments or must be guaranteed by a government. IDA credits are made to governments only.

The purpose of IFC is to assist the economic development of less developed countries by promoting growth in the private sector of their economies and helping to mobilize domestic and foreign capital for this purpose.

The relative importance of the three institutions is indicated by the 1981 fiscal year totals. IBRD made loans for a total of $8,809 million, IDA granted credits for a total of $3,482 million, IFC made equity and loan commitments for a total of $811 million.

John A. Holsen states that "The World Bank Group has no set formula for creditworthiness analysis."[3] However, he mentions at least three broad classes of countries from the point of view of creditworthiness:

[1]Stephen H. Goodman. "Financing and Risk in Developing Countries," In *Proceedings of a Symposium on Developing Countries' Debt*. Sponsored by The Export-Import Bank of the United States, August 1977; Introduction: An Overview of Financing and Risk in Developing Countries, p. 2.
[2]*World Bank Annual Report 1981*, p. 3.
[3]John A. Holsen. "Financing and Risk in Developing Countries." In *Proceedings of a Symposium on Developing Countries' Debt*. Sponsored by the Export-Import Bank of the United States, August 1977; Chapter 13, World Bank Techniques for Country Evaluation, p. 99.

1) those we consider not currently creditworthy for regular World Bank loans but which are eligible for "soft" IDA credits;
2) those which we consider fully creditworthy for the approved amount of "hard" Bank lending; and
3) those with limited creditworthiness for Bank financing, which consequently receive varying blends of "hard" and "soft" resources.[4]

Holsen adds that there are exceptionally, also a few countries which are creditworthy for Bank lending, but to which IDA provides credits (alone or in combination with Bank resources) simply on the grounds of their poverty. One should add two other categories:

— those countries where either "economic performance" or project preparation is insufficient to justify any financing on either "hard" or "soft" term, and
— those countries that are sufficiently well established in the capital markets that they no longer require financing from the World Bank Group.[5]

The World Bank does not publish country ratings, but the ratings may be derived from the annual report appendices "Bank and IDA Cumulative Lending Operations, by Borrower or Guarantor"

PRACTICAL COUNTRY CLASSIFICATION

By comparing the cumulative IBRD loans and/or IDA credits listed in two different annual reports, one finds out whether a country has received loans or credits during the intervening period, and how much.

This information may be used for creditworthiness purposes by subdividing countries into various groups, for instance:

I. Countries that have not received IBRD loans or IDA credits during the preceding five years.

II. Countries that have received IBRD loans but not IDA credits during the preceding five years.

III. Countries that have received both IBRD loans and IDA credits during the preceding five years.

IV. Countries that have received only IDA credits during the preceding five years.

4Ibid., p. 99.
5Ibid., p. 99.

The classification broadly reflects the World Bank's opinion about each country's ability, or inability, to borrow from private sources. The selection of a five-year period is, of course, arbitrary; it could be one year, three years, or any period which the analyst deems to be significant.

Table 6 lists 116 countries subdivided into the above mentioned groups on the basis of their getting, or not getting loans or credits from IBRD or IDA during the five-year period from June 30, 1976 to June 30, 1981.

As an indication of their market size for international banking, the countries are listed in order of their 1980 "gross external revenues (GER)."

Table 6   Classification of Countries on the Basis of their Using—Or Not Using—World Bank Credits Or Loans During the Five Year Period 6/30/1976 and 6/30/1981, with Indication of their 1980 "Gross External Revenues (GER)"—Million SDRs.

Country	1980 GER	Country	1980 GER
Group I—Countries that did not receive IDA credits or IBRD loans during the period.			
United States	266,080	Kuwait	21,586
Germany	187,300	Australia	20,566
United Kingdom	129,639	Iraq	20,267*
France	128,196	Singapore	18,762
Japan	121,930	Denmark	18,441
Italy	84,269	Venezuela	17,186
Saudi Arabia	83,898	Finland	13,419
Netherlands	75,771	Libya	12,765
Belgium	69,599	Iran	10,983*
Canada	61,056	Israel	10,076
Switzerland	33,394	Ireland	7,792
Sweden	29,806	New Zealand	5,018
Austria	23,006	Gabon	1,624
So. Africa	22,700	Iceland	946
Norway	21,864	Malta	940
Group II—Countries that received IBRD loans but did not receive IDA credits during the period.			
Spain	27,999	Tunisia	2,678
Nigeria	19,529	Oman	2,583

(continued)

Table 6 (Continued)

Country	1980 GER	Country	1980 GER
Mexico	19,280	Ecuador	2,278
Brazil	18,134	Trinidad & Tobago	1,733
So. Korea	17,809	Panama	1,678
Algeria	11,526	Guatemala	1,505
Malaysia	11,158	El Salvador	1,171
Yugoslavia	10,820	Jamaica	1,220
Argentina	8,668	Dominican Rep.	993
Portugal	7,590	Uruguay	973
Greece	7,279	Costa Rica	956
Turkey	4,913	Bahamas	894
Chile	4,804	Cyprus	892
Colombia	4,387	Botswana	670
Morocco	3,463	Paraguay	538
Peru	3,286	Fiji	487
Syria	3,247	Mauritius	473
Ivory Coast	2,690	Barbados	465
		Swaziland	344

Group III—Countries that received both IBRD loans and IDA credits during the
     period.

Indonesia	17,097	Senegal	877
India	8,111	Bolivia	859
Egypt	7,138	Congo Peoples Rep.	856
Thailand	6,606	Honduras	762
Philippines	6,381	Tanzania	663
Pakistan	4,479	Sudan	658
Jordan	2,945	Nicaragua	585
Kenya	1,673	Liberia	462*

(continued)

Table 6 *(Continued)*

Country	1980 GER	Country	1980 GER
Zimbabwe	1,401	Guyana	316
Cameroon	1,385	Mali	316
Zambia	1,076	Malawi	281
Papua N.G.	1,061	Upper Volta	279
Ghana	1,046	Mauritania	267

Group IV—Countries that received only IDA credits during the period.

Country	1980 GER	Country	1980 GER
Bangladesh	1,651	Nepal	285
Yemen Arab Rep.	1,398	Niger	279
Zaire	1,290	Rwanda	248
Sri Lanka	1,252	Central Afr. Rep.	235
Ethiopia	497	Benin Peoples Rep.	229
Burma	441	Sierra Leone	217
Madagascar	440	Togo	204
Yemen Peoples Rep.	356	Chad	82
Haiti	346	Gambia	76
Uganda	329	Burundi	51*
Somalia	311	Lesotho	48*
		Western Samoa	19

Summary
Total "gross external revenues (GER)" (million SDRs)

Group I	1,518,879
Group II	209,113
Group III	67,580
Group IV	10,284
Total sample	1,805,856

*Merchandise exports from IFS.
Source: World Bank Annual Report, 1976 and 1981; Balance of Payments Statistics, Vol. 32.

The countries that interest private lenders are, first, those that did not borrow either from IBRD or IDA (Group I), and next, countries that were considered fully creditworthy for IBRD loans (Group II). Together these two groups account for 95.4 percent of global "gross external revenues."[6]

Group III countries that were considered creditworthy for IBRD loans but also received IDA credits on account of their poverty account for 3.7 percent of global GER.

The 23 countries in Group IV which are not considered creditworthy for IBRD loans and countries not listed in the World Bank report accounted for less than one percent of global GER.

When considering World Bank classifications, one should keep in mind the great temptation represented by a 50-year IDA credit with a 10-year grace period at a 0.75 percent annual charge. Also, a 20-year IBRD loan with a 5-year grace period at market-related interest rates is worth trying for.

One may thus assume that applicants for loans or credits would be inclined to present a rather poor picture of their situation, and since the World Bank staff is probably inclined to help applicants, one may conclude that in some instances a country's creditworthiness is better than its World Bank classification. At any rate World Bank classifications should be taken into consideration.

It is debatable whether a bank should spend time and money for credit-worthiness evaluations of the 23 countries in the group which generated less than 0.6 percent of global foreign exchange. From a practical viewpoint, a bank may decide to lend modest amounts of money to very poor countries and perhaps consider such amounts implicitly as promotion expenditures.

---

[6]*Balance of Payments Statistics*, Vol. 32, Part 2, p. 40. Global Merchandise FOB 1,288, Other Goods Services and Income 459, Private and Official Unrequited Transfers 57, Total 1980 GER 1,804 billion SDRs.

chapter 11

Selection of Evaluation Procedure

A. Bruce Brackenridge remarked in 1977 "I was also fascinated that bankers in the 1920s used almost exactly the same basic factors in determining creditworthiness that are being used by most international lenders today."[1]

But conditions in the international lending field have changed completely during the last 50 years:

— foreign bonds, due in 20 or 30 years, represented almost all international borrowing in the 1920s, while today bank lending, mostly short- and medium-term, predominates; moreover,

— practically no data were available in the 1920s on the external accounts of the borrowing countries, while today thousands of data are published by the IMF, the World Bank, the OECD, the United Nations, central banks, commercial banks, and so on.

When loans were prevalently of 20 to 30 years' duration, with initial grace periods frequently of five years or more during which no principal amortization was paid, the terms of the bonds allowed enough time for economic development to take place. It was reasonable to appraise loans on a country's economic growth basis.

[1]A. Bruce Brackenridge, "Financing and Risk in Developing Countries." In *Proceedings of a Symposium on Developing Countries' Debt*. Sponsored by the Export-Import Bank of the United States, August 1977; Chapter 9, One Approach to Country Evaluation, p. 76.

On the other hand, a subjective evaluation of a prospective borrower's domestic situation was the only evaluation that could be made because data on external accounts were practically non-existent at that time.

In view of changed conditions, it is suggested that the creditworthiness evaluation should start with an analysis of the external account, based on factual, comparable data. That should be followed by an evaluation of domestic, social, political, and economic conditions, giving due consideration to exogenous factors. However, the analysis of factual comparable data of the external accounts should be the foundation of a country's evaluation.

EXTERNAL REPAYMENT CAPABILITY

The keystone of the suggested evaluation approach is the external repayment capability. A relatively good external repayment capability does not automatically signify a good credit risk, but, if the repayment capability is relatively poor, then the credit risk is relatively less desirable, unless unusual favorable developments are forecast.

External repayment capability is essentially composed of three elements:

1. Relative foreign exchange generating capability indicator based on:
   — increases of foreign exchange earnings during recent periods
   — foreign exchange earnings' instability index
   — foreign exchange earnings' concentration index.

2. Relative overspending habits indicator, consisting of the following elements:
   — current account imbalance as percentage of gross external revenues (GER) during recent periods
   — current account imbalance as percentage of GER increases during recent period.

3. Relative external financial burden indicator, consisting of the following elements:
   — imbalance between external debit and credit interest as percentage of GER during recent periods
   — imbalance between external debit and credit interest, plus imbalance between profits due and receivable on foreign equity investments as percentage of GER during recent periods.

The reader will notice that all indicators are based on gross external revenues denominators and not on gross domestic product denominators. The reasons are explained in Chapter 5, under "GDP or GNP Denominators."

The analysis of each one of the three elements is essential for the evaluation of a country's external repayment capability.

Any repayment of external debts is predicated on the availability of foreign exchange, or to be more precise, on the ability to generate foreign exchange in the future. It is, therefore, essential to determine whether external revenues are increasing in a satisfactory manner, moreover, to determine how steady such earnings were in the past, and finally to try to estimate their vulnerability to exogenous factors. These subjects are discussed in detail in Chapter 15, GROSS EXTERNAL REVENUES (GER).

On the other hand, overspending habits can absorb any amount of foreign exchange earned leaving nothing for the repayment of external debts. Therefore, the relationship between deficits in current account (which reflect overspending) and total foreign exchange revenues, and the relationship between current account deficits and increases of foreign exchange revenues, are discussed in Chapter 14, CURRENT ACCOUNT.

Finally, the foreign exchange generating capability may show satisfactory increases, and overspending abroad may be within reasonable limits, but the burden of existing external debts may be so heavy as to make their repayment extremely difficult. This is discussed in Chapter 16, FINANCIAL INCOME AND EXPENDITURES (Investment Income).

The practical application of the indicators is tested in Chapter 19, EXPERIMENTAL TESTING—CONCLUSIONS.

LIQUIDITY PROBLEMS

The weaknesses of liquidity indicators based on offical reserves are discussed in Chapter 6, LIQUIDITY PROBLEMS.

The following ratios should be tried in addition to reserve-based ratios:

1. Interest earned on international assets as percentage of interest due on external debts (see Chapter 16 FINANCIAL INCOME AND EXPENDITURES).
2. Balances of a country and its residents with banks reporting to the Bank for International Settlements (BIS) as percentage of the amounts due by each country and its residents to the same banks (see Chapter 6, under "Credit Balances Held With and Amounts Borrowed From Banks").

Each one of the two ratios has its weak point. The first one is calculated on the basis of Balance of Payments Statistics data, which become available with a time lag of at least one year and which is quite long for a liquidity indicator. The second ratio gives only a partial picture of the situation because it reflects only balances held with, or amounts due to, banks reporting to the BIS. That means that debts due to official lenders are not included in the computation.

Both ratios throw more light on the situation. They indicate whether a country has international assets—besides reserves—that may be available in case of emergency, or whether a country is, so to say, scraping the bottom of the barrel (see Chapter 19 EXPERIMENTAL TESTING—CONCLUSIONS).

PER CAPITA INCOMES INCREASES AND POPULATION INCREASES

Per capita incomes should be taken into consideration in the creditworthiness evaluation. Their level is the most comprehensive indicator of a country's economic development. Stagnating, or declining, per capita incomes portend future political difficulties for a country's authorities and consequently the likelihood of actions which may damage external creditors (see Chapter 17, PER CAPITA INCOMES AND POPULATION INCREASES, and Chapter 19 EXPERIMENTAL TESTING—CONCLUSIONS).

High birth rates which cause rapid population increases are among the most intractable problems of developing countries.

PRIVATE BORROWERS

Procedures for the evaluation of the additional risk incurred when lending abroad to non-official borrowers, or without an offical guarantee, cannot be standardized because problems vary from country to country.

The most damaging eventualities affecting private borrowers are new currency transfer restrictions and deep currency devaluations. Transfer restrictions could be subsequently relaxed, but the damage caused by a deep currency devaluation to a non-official borrower is permanent.

The subject is discussed in Chapter 12 PRIVATE BORROWERS. The ratio suggested as a warning signal is "Dollar Adjusted CPI Increase as Percentage of Dollar Rate of Exchange Increase."

SUGGESTED OUTLINE OF REPORT

Most observers agree with William R. Cline that "It would seem that whether a country is going to be forced to default or to reschedule is essentially an economic question. It should be subject to analysis by focusing on the key economic variables which determine the likelihood of default.[2]

[2]William R. Cline, op. cit., Chapter 14, Panel Discussion: Managing and Assessing Developing Country Risk, p. 111

Therefore, the emphasis of the evaluation should be on economic factors and the report submitted to management should reflect that fact.

The report should consist of four sections:

— Comparable Factual Data
— Judgmental Economic Factors
— Judgmental Social and Political Factors
— Conclusions[3]

This arrangement shows to what extent the evaluation is based on comparable data or on subjective judgments about noncomparable factors.

The following factors should be included in the Comparable Factual Data profile:

— relative external repayment capability indicator
— relative liquidity indicator
— relative per capita increase and population increase indicator
— relative loss of domestic currency purchasing power indicator (particularly relevant when private borrowers are involved).

These elements are the foundation on which a country's creditworthiness evaluation should be based.

The report should specifically state whether some variables or ratios are based on estimates because data needed to complete the profile are missing. Unusual delays in the release of data should be pointed out in the report because some authorities are inclined to delay the publication of unfavorable information.

What should be included in the two judgmental sections is a matter of preference. In general, one may suggest that

— comments should be short,
— the emphasis should be on factors affecting the external accounts, and
— a uniform format should be followed.

Sound, understandable concepts should be used for the selection of factors or variables to be included in the creditworthiness evaluation. Equally important is the selection of sound procedures and techniques to be used in the evaluation process.

---

[3]Bank of America uses a similar outline: Debt Service Capacity Index, Judgmental Economic Indicator, and Judgmental Political Indicator. See also Chapter 9, STRUCTURED SYSTEMS: OUTLINES AND MODELS.

LONG-RANGE PERFORMANCE

One of the concepts underlying the creditworthiness evaluation procedure suggested in this book is that a country's agricultural, industrial, commercial, and financial structure, and its social and political institutions are the result of many years of development, and, as such, should not be expected to change suddenly except in case of revolutionary events.

Since past performance is the result of a country's structural characteristics and institutions, it is reasonable moreover to assume that, on average, there is a more than even chance that past performance will not be subject to sudden drastic changes. "On average" does not mean that each country's future performance will continue to reflect the past. It means that as a group countries that performed better in the past will outperform countries that performed poorly.

Therefore, long-range past performance should be taken as the foundation on which a country's creditworthiness evaluation should be built. As stated in Chapter 4 under "Social and Political Factors," the analyst should evaluate and compare results (performance) rather than causes (structural characteristics and institutions).

RANKING SYSTEMS AND RELATIVE INDICATORS

The lack of definable thresholds dividing performance ratios of acceptable risks from unacceptable risks is discussed in Chapter 3 under "No Definable Thresholds". The few indicative thresholds mentioned in Chapter 9, under "Indicative Thresolds" should be considered as examples rather than limits.

In the absence of defined thresholds ratios indicate only relative performance and are useful for ranking countries with the purpose of identifying those with higher and more imminent probability of payment difficulties. Incidentally, the search for reliable overall creditworthiness rating systems reflects the awareness of most analysts that evaluations should be made on a relative basis.

In most country ranking systems, the variables used in the evaluation are arranged in declining order from best to worst, and scores are assigned on the basis of the place of each variable. The scores are then combined to obtain an overall rating.

That would be fine if ratios deteriorated uniformly, for instance, from 100 to 99, then to 98 and 97, and so on, in a sample of 100 countries. However, in practice the deterioration is not uniform; frequently two or more countries have the same ratios, or ratios may deteriorate suddenly.

The following example illustrates the point. It is part of Table 9 in Chapter 14 reporting the 1980 ratios of Current Account Imbalance as Percentage of Gross External Revenues (GER) for a sample of 51 countries.

Scores based on each country's place do not reflect their relative ratios,

Place in Table	Country	Ratio	Relative Indicator*
15	Germany	6.5	59
16	Belgium	6.5	59
17	Iceland	6.6	59
18	Israel	6.7	60
19	Japan	6.8	61
20	Finland	8.0	72
21	Guatemala	8.3	75
22	Italy	8.9	80
23	Tunisia	9.2	83

*Median of sample; i.e., 11.1, equals 100.

since ratios increase by 5 percent within 4 places from 6.5 to 6.8 and increase by 35 percent in the next 4 places from 6.8 to 9.2. A deterioration of 5 percent and one of 35 percent would be both indicated by a four-point drop in rating if place rankings were used.

More troublesome is that place rankings do not indicate to what extent the performance of countries at the bottom of the list is worse than the median performance of countries included in a sample.

For instance, Table 13, "Gross External Revenues (GER) Instability Index," places Venezuela at the bottom of the list with a relative instability index of 320, while Costa Rica is placed at the bottom of Table 10, "Current Account Imbalance as Percentage of GER Increase" with a relative indicator of 1627. On the basis of place rankings both variables would be added with the same score (last on list) in an overall ranking computation, although Costa Rica's current account deficit ratio is 16 times worse than the median of the sample, while Venezuela's GER instability indicator is only three times worse than the median.

To overcome such inconsistencies, variables to be included in composite ratings should be calculated on a relative indicator basis in which 100 represents the median of the sample used (that is the procedure followed in Chapter 19, EXPERIMENTAL TESTING—CONCLUSIONS).

Medians change of course from period to period, meaning that the basis of relative indicators will also change. Needless to say, averages could be used instead of medians; that is a subjective decision.

SELECTION OF BASE PERIOD

One of the most perplexing problems in the creditworthiness evaluation process is the selection of the period of time on which the evaluation is based. The period should be long enough to reflect basic conditions, but it should not be too long because the observations made could be invalidated by subsequent events.

First, one should avoid the danger of being pulled into the "last minute news" vortex. Last minute news may be useful in stock or commodity trading, but adds only confusion if one were to try to use it as basis for creditworthiness evaluation.

Creditworthiness of a corporation does not change with every quarterly increase or drop of its profits and, of course, not with every change of its stock quotation. Similarly, the creditworthiness of a country does not change with every month-to-month or quarter-to-quarter variation of its exports or imports, or reserves, or the daily fluctuations of the rate of exchange of its currency. Yet the temptation to update and change continuously every assessment or projection is hard to resist. It almost seems as if the availability of instant global information and of computers that can quickly work out complicated models creates the need for a stream of up-to-the-minute reports (another aspect of Parkinson's Law?).

On the other hand, it would be absurd to ignore the latest developments; but they should not be taken in isolation or form the principal basis for credit-worthiness evaluation.

The selection of the length of the base period is essentially a subjective decision, based on common sense and past experience.

A special problem arises when one wants to calculate, for instance, an instability index. A ten-year base period is advisable for that purpose, because the period should be long enough to include two international trade slowdowns. Many things change in ten years and the long base period weakens the reliability of the index. A shorter period, however, may reflect only fair weather perform-ance (see Chapter 15, under "GER Instability Index").

MULTIPLE EVALUATIONS

Creditworthiness evaluations are usually expressed by one rating. Since the evaluation is based on past performance and forecasts of future trends of a number of variables, one rating implies that the analyst has found one basic underlying trend for each variable involved and is, moreover, confident that such trends will continue.

As anyone familiar with statistics knows, it is practically impossible to find a statistical series that shows a steady and constant trend over any period of time long enough to be accepted as evidence of basic trend. The phenomena reflected by any statistic are subject to all kinds of variations: incidental, cyclical, or secular. Different base periods will inevitably lead to different results. Management, however, traditionally wants one definite rating, or firm opinion. As a result the analyst either selects subjectively one period as being representative of the basic situation or, more probably, averages data of several periods and submits one single rating or opinion. What happens is that the analyst is forced to make a final guestimate, and management is under the illusion of having an unequivocal evaluation.

One way of overcoming such difficulties is to use data of various periods, for instance, 3, 2, and 1 year, calculate ratios for each period, and then select the lower and higher ratios as representing the range of the evaluation.

For example, Table 12, "Gross External Revenues (GER) Percentage Increase," in SDR terms shows, for Japan:

	1978/1980	1979/1980	1980
Relative Indicators	84	74	141
Which reflect yearly percentage increases of	14.0%	15.5%	24.0%
Against median increase of countries in sample of	16.7%	21.0%	17.0%

The lower indicator of 74 and the higher indicator of 141 are included in the calculation of the "factual repayment risk indicator" (see Chapter 19 EXPERIMENTAL TESTING—CONCLUSIONS).

Management may be unhappy with such suggestions, but should be aware that a sound foundation for one specific evaluation is lacking because the selection of procedures is judgmental, the assessment of political and social factors is judgmental, trends on which the evaluation is based vary from period to period, and the assignment of weights to each factor is judgmental.

Differences of opinion or interpretation are inevitable. A consensus evaluation only means that judgmental differences have been "swept under the rug." That is counterproductive; management should insist upon being informed of such differences of opinion because they reflect the extent of the uncertainty of the evaluation.

How a system using multiple evaluations works in practice is tested in Chapter 19, EXPERIMENTAL TESTING—CONCLUSIONS.

WEIGHTS

The problem of assigning a weight to each variable arises whenever more than one variable is involved in the evaluation and that is, of course, always the case.

Apart from the impossibility of measuring human factors—in the social and political field—the problem of weighing factual variables is the biggest obstacle if one wishes to set up an overall creditworthiness rating system.

After attributing weights to each variable, the components have to be added up in order to obtain the final rating. That means that under certain circumstances, a good rating could reflect disastrous circumstances.

J. Alexander Caldwell and J. Antonio Villamil explain the problem: "Suppose, for example, that political stability received a weight of 20 percent out of 100 percent in a system where average creditworthiness is thought to be around 60 percent. In such case Iran may still appear to be of adequate creditworthiness—even with the political component valued at zero."[4]

The biggest problem is the subjective nature of any weighing system. It is obvious that different weights, as already stated, change the valuation outcome. Some analysts try to reduce the subjective element by using a double scoring system in which weighed scores are compared with unweighed ones. That is a step in the right direction because it points out the uncertainty of the evaluations.

No overall creditworthiness ranking calculations will be attempted in this study because no satisfactory weighing system has been found.

As an example of procedures to be explored, a "factual repayment risk indicator," representing seven variables, is shown in Chapter 19, EXPERIMENTAL TESTING—CONCLUSIONS.

[4]J. Alexander Caldwell and J. Antonio Villamil. *Assessing Country Risk.* Euromoney Publications, London, 1981; Chapter 1, Factors Affecting Creditworthiness, p. 20.

chapter 12

Private Borrowers

Lending abroad to businesses, corporations, or banks involves special risks which do not arise when lending to a government or making a loan with government guarantee (see Chapter 2 under "Commercial Risk").

The most serious and hard to predict problems affecting the repayment of private external debts are new currency transfer restrictions and difficulties caused by severe currency devaluations.

EXCHANGE RESTRICTIONS

The private borrower may have the domestic currency needed to pay his obligations but may be unable to obtain the foreign exchange needed to pay foreign creditors, or he may have the foreign exchange needed to pay his external obligation but may be prevented from transferring the funds abroad by foreign exchange restrictions in force in his country (see Chapter 2, under "Transfer Risk").

The *Annual Report—Exchange Arrangements and Exchange Restrictions* published by the IMF, lists the exchange restrictions in force in countries which are members of the Fund. The Report consists of two parts and an Analytical Appendix.

Part One traces the main developments in restrictive practices, including restrictions on imports and import payments, measures affecting exports, restrictions on current invisibles, multiple currency practices, bilateral payments agreements, and measures affecting the transfer of capital. This part also provides a brief review of economic developments during the year and a description of changes in regional arrangements during the period.

Part Two, the bulk of the Report, includes country by country surveys of the exchange and trade restrictions of individual members.

The report probably deserves more attention than it has traditionally received from analysts. Special attention should be given to the last section of the country surveys "changes during the period."

The imposition of new, or stricter, restrictions is usually a symptom of a deteriorating situation; conversely, the removal, or mitigation, or restrictions is usually a favorable sign.

Such changes, however, indicate only how local authorities perceive their country's situation, and that may be overly optimistic or pessimistic. The 1979 Report, for instance, shows that Mexico eliminated import licensing requirements for about two thirds of the items in the customs classification, indicating that the Mexican authorities were optimistic about the future outlook of the country's external accounts.

In some instances foreign exchange regulations are kept in force by bureaucratic habit. A good example is Britain. For 40 years (1939 to 1979) British residents were allowed only a limited amount of foreign exchange for travel abroad, they could not buy or sell gold bullion, they could not buy or sell foreign exchange without an official authorization, and so on. The pound touched its lowest point in 1976. By the end of 1977, however, the situation had turned around completely. Britain's "Total Reserves, Minus Gold" had increased to such embarrassingly high levels that only Germany and Japan had higher "Total Reserves, Minus Gold." It took the British Conservative government almost two years to decide that exchange restrictions had outlived their usefulness (the opposition Labor Party strongly criticized the removal of transfer restrictions).

IMPOSITION OF NEW OR TIGHTER RESTRICTIONS

The possibility that existing foreign exchange restrictions may be tightened or that new restrictions may be imposed is frequently considered a political risk; however, its causes are essentially economic. Restrictions are not imposed to spite foreigners; they are enacted because a country is short of foreign exchange.

Deteriorating foreign exchange flows are reflected in a country's external accounts. Any forecast, however, as to whether or when new restrictions may be enacted, or old ones tightened, is a matter of judgmental speculation. One thing is sure: the probability becomes higher and more imminent if the external accounts continue to deteriorate.

CURRENCY DEVALUATIONS

For creditworthiness evaluation purposes a currency devaluation can be seen from two opposing viewpoints: A private debtor will no doubt be handicapped by a devaluation since it will take a greater amount of local currency to repay a foreign debt. A debtor country, on the other hand, may be helped by a devaluation, especially if its currency was overvalued.

Currency devaluations are usually expressed in percentages. For example, if the value of one unit of local currency was equal to one dollar and is subsequently reduced to 50 cents, there is a 50 percent devaluation. But the private debtor who used to get one dollar for each local currency unit will subsequently have to pay twice as much in local currency. For a private borrower, a 50 percent currency devaluation means a 100 percent increase in servicing burden.

Recent events in Mexico have emphasized the problem. At the rate of 70 pesos to the dollar (September 1982) a debtor needed almost three times the amount of pesos required twelve months before the devaluation to pay his dollar debts.

The events in Mexico are not unique. The rate of exchange of the Argentine peso went from 60.9 to the dollar at the end of 1975 to 274.5 at the end of 1976. Within twelve months a private debtor needed four and one half times as many pesos to pay his dollar obligations.

In the normal course of events local inflation precedes devaluation so that in local currency terms the business turnover (and presumably the ability to service debt) of a debtor should expand with inflation. But it is highly unlikely that a debtor whose income is mainly in local currency could cope with a three- or fourfold increase in servicing charges.

In addition to the usual credit analysis one should determine how much of a private borrower's income is represented by foreign exchange, which will not be affected by local devaluations.

Another factor which adversely affects private borrowers is domestic recession. If the economies of other countries continue to expand, the balance of payments of the debtor's country may improve, enhancing in the short run the public sector's external debt-service ability, whereas a recession may cause severe payments problems in the private sector.

HOW PROBABLE IS A DEVALUATION?

The big question is of course: What are the probabilities that the local currency may be depreciated in terms of the currency in which the debt is denominated?

Although no definitive answer can be given to that question, there are nonetheless some symptoms that indicate increased or decreased devaluation probabilities. Among them:

— exceptional declines in reserves,

— substantial and persistent deficit in the current account, and

— decline in the purchasing power of a country's currency not reflected in the foreign exchange rate.

EXCEPTIONAL DECLINES IN RESERVES

If the reserves of a country suffer a deep decline, the monetary authorities may decide that a devaluation of the currency is inevitable. Moreover, if the decline is part of a liquidity crisis, and if IMF aid is asked for, the Fund may find that the currency is overvalued and require a devaluation as part of a lending package.

Some destabilizing factors that affect the level of reserves are listed in the following paragraphs.

Leads and lags in the settlement of foreign trade obligations usually aggravate a liquidity crisis. When a devaluation of a currency is anticipated, exporters will try to hold on to the foreign currency, perhaps even granting longer payment terms, while importers will try to pay as soon as possible or hedge through forward contracts.

In industrial countries capital movements from one financial center to another add to the instability of the overall balance of payments, with consequent fluctuations in the official reserves. That may be caused by various factors.

There may be a difference in real return—interest rates less inflationary price increases—between currencies, so that an international investor may buy a currency as an asset which he expects to appreciate. Or the interest rate differential on deposits in various currencies, adjusted for the spread of their respective spot and forward quotations, may make a switch profitable.

SUBSTANTIAL AND PERSISTENT CURRENT ACCOUNT DEFICITS

The overall creditworthiness problems created by substantial and persistent current account deficits are discussed in Chapter 14 CURRENT ACCOUNT.

An overvalued currency is one of the causes of current account deficits. However even if the currency is actually not overvalued, the authorities may decide that that is the cause of the deficits and devalue it anyway. Or, as already mentioned, if IMF assistance is asked, the Fund may suggest that the currency should be devalued.

In most instances persistent current account deficits erode the level of reserves, and that may precipitate a devaluation.

CHANGES OF A CURRENCY'S RELATIVE PURCHASING POWER

Exchange rate adjustments seldom follow month-to-month or quarter-to-quarter changes of the purchasing power of a currency. In the long run, however, inflation will be reflected in subsequent exchange rate adjustments.

A currency becomes progressively overvalued if exchange rate adjustments don't follow domestic price increases, and that leads subsequently to deep devaluations which place private borrowers with foreign exchange debts in great difficulty.

Private borrowers and their foreign creditors who are adversely affected by currency devaluations should look for any diverging trends between domestic inflation levels and exchange rate adjustments. More specifically, they should

Table 7   Dollar Adjusted CPI Increase as Percentage of Dollar Rate of Exchange Increase—1978/1980 (Relative Purchasing Power Indicator).

Egypt	63	Turkey	103
Indonesia	80	Zambia	103
Germany	83	Australia	104
Switzerland	83	Ecuador	104
Belgium	84	France	105
Austria	86	Malta	105
Brazil	86	Sri Lanka	105
Netherlands	86	Sweden	105
Malaysia	87	Thailand	105
Canada	88	Ireland	108
Norway	89	New Zealand	108
Tunisia	91	Venezuela	111
Jamaica	95	Colombia	112
Japan	95	Philippines	112
Morocco	95	Italy	113
Pakistan	95	Kenya	114
Syria	95	Israel	119
Guatemala	97	So. Africa	123
Finland	99	Tanzania	126
Iceland	99	Spain	127
United States	100	Bolivia	130
Greece	100	Mexico	137
Costa Rica)	101	Paraguay	138
Honduras	102	United Kingdom	138
So. Korea	102	Chile	156
Cyprus	103		

Source: *IFS*, December 1981.

follow closely changes in the "dollar adjusted inflation rate"—measured by the differential between local and U.S. inflation rates—and compare such changes with adjustments of the exchange rate of the local currency against the dollar.

The main problem with this approach is that, as a rule, the purchasing power of a currency declines steadily while, in most instances, exchange rates are adjusted occasionally. This lack of synchronization between the two phenomena makes comparisons difficult. To compensate partially for the lack of concurrence, the calculation should cover a period of several years.

Since consumer prices indexes (CPI) are widely available, with relatively short time lags, they are used in this book as representing inflationary levels.

Table 7 shows "Dollar Adjusted CPI Increase as Percentage of Dollar Rate of Exchange Increase" during the period 1978 to 1980 for 51 countries.

An index of less than 100 indicates a trend toward a relative purchasing power under-valuation; conversely an index higher than 100 indicates a trend toward over-valuation. By definition, the United States will have an index of 100.

Table 8 Mexico—Disparities Between Dollar Adjusted CPI Increases and Dollar Exchange Rate Changes.

	Mexico CPI (1)	U.S.A. CPI (2)	Mexico/USA Index (3)	Mexico/USA Exchange Rate (4)	(3) Divided by (4) (5)
1971	100	100	100	100	100
1972	105	103	102	100	102
1973	118	110	107	100	107
1974	146	122	120	100	120
1975	168	133	126	100	126
After 1976 devaluation (new indexes)					
1976	100	100	100	100	100
1977	129	107	120	114	105
1978	151	115	131	114	115
1979	179	128	140	114	123
1980	226	145	156	117	133
1981*	296	162	183	125	146

*August
Source: *IFS 1981 Yearbook, IFS, December 1981.*

Table 7 should be taken with a grain of salt; a three-year period is rather short for this kind of calculation.

Of the five countries at the bottom of the list Bolivia devalued 85 percent, Chile 47 percent and Mexico 76 percent in the next two years while the British pound declined by one third against the U.S. dollar. Only the Paraguayan guaranty/U.S. dollar rate remained unchanged in the following two years.

More significant is Table 8 showing the disparities between dollar adjusted consumer prices increases and Mexican peso/U.S. dollar rate exchange increases during the five years preceeding the 1976 peso devaluation and the five years preceeding the 1982 devaluation.

Mexico's example leaves no doubt about the importance of detecting sub-stantial disparities between dollar adjusted CPI increases (column 3) and dollar exchange rate increases (column 4). Substantial disparities should be considered as warning signals of trouble ahead. See Chapter 19, EXPERIMENTAL TEST-ING—CONCLUSIONS.

chapter 13

Balance of Payments

Any comprehensive evaluation of external country creditworthiness should start with an analysis of the information contained in the yearly *Balance of Payments Statistics* (BPS) and its monthly supplements published by the IMF.

Yet, strangely, the *Balance of Payments Statistics* are seldom mentioned among sources of information for external accounts data. Alexander McW. Wolfe, Jr., for instance, mentions that ". . . balance-of-payments figures . . . are reported in the monthly publication International Financial Statistics."[1]

International Financial Statistics (IFS) reports only a sketchy summary consisting of:

6 current account entries
4 capital account entries
1 Net Errors and Omissions entry (see below) and
5 entries related to reserves (mostly irrelevant for a country's performance evaluation).

The data appearing in the IFS are only a summary of data published in the BPS monthly supplements. The IFS is a collection of mostly unrelated

[1]Alexander Mc W. Wolfe, Jr. *Offshore Lending by U.S. Commercial Banks.* Bankers' Association for Foreign Trade, Washington, D.C. and Robert Morris Associates, Philadelphia, Pa., 1981; Chapter 2, International Lending Risks, Part I: Country Risk, under Balance of Payments, p. 44.

statistics. For example, increases or decreases of reserves, of merchandise exports, or imports are not tied in with other data. The analyst does not know the meaning of changes reported. Yet the IFS enjoys great popularity among analysts.

The popularity may be explained only by the frequency of publication of the IFS. Some analysts seem to believe that it is preferable to have a great deal of up-to-date information rather than less recent basic data.

The Balance of Payments Statistics, on the other hand, is an orderly presentation in which each entry must have its counterpart. For instance, the origin of the funds for reserve increases of more than one hundred percent shown by Paraguay, Ghana, and Costa Rica during the two years 1977 to 1978, mentioned in Chapter 6, under "Accumulation of External Debts and Level of Reserves," turns out to be new borrowing (see "Aggregate Presentation" in the following pages.)

The Detailed Presentation of the yearly *Balance of Payments Statistics* includes a total of 112 items of which:

    44   pertaining to the current account
    53   pertaining to the capital account
    14   pertaining to reserves
     1   Net Errors and Omissions (N.E. & O.)

This gold mine of information will be discussed in this chapter and in Chapters 14, 15, and 16.

DEFINITION

In order to use the information intelligently, the analyst should know the assumptions on which the compilation of the balance of payments is based and the meaning of the concepts and terms used in it.

As to what the balance of payments is, the *Balance of Payments Manual* (hereafter referred to as *Manual*) offers the following definition:

> "A balance of payments statement can be broadly described as the record
> of an economy's international economic transactions, that is, of the goods
> and services that an economy has received from and provided to the rest of
> the world and of the changes in the economy's claims on and liabilities to
> the rest of the world."[2]

In other words, the balance of payments is a record of the country's economic dealings with the rest of the world. From a practical point of view, it reflects the country's foreign exchange flows.

---

[2]*Balance of Payments Manual, IMF, Fourth Edition.* International Monetary Fund, 1977; Introduction, p. 1.

To maximize intercountry comparability, all country statistics are based on the same concepts and are compiled in a uniform way.

The balance of payments must balance. Imbalances in a country's current account (the difference between external revenues and external expenditures) must be offset by long-term and short-term capital transfers or changes in official reserves.

TERMINOLOGY

The *Manual* states:

> "The terminology that has been applied in this Manual to identify various balances is not likely to be very illuminating to users who are not already familiar with the concepts concerned. For one thing, the same balance may sometimes be described by reference either to the components above the line or to those below the line, as in the so-called overall balance or official settlements balance. Moreover, the same term is often used to cover two or more similar but not identical versions of a particular concept. In practice, therefore, it is desirable to specify precisely the components of any balance that is being employed."[3]

For those not familiar with balance of payments terminology, one may add that "above the line" means all items included in the computation of the kind of balance of payments taken into consideration, and "below the line" means the items excluded from the computation.

The *Manual* also points out that

> "For one thing, some of the most fundamental concepts are complicated and cannot be described solely in terms of well-defined characteristics that could be discerned readily or of rules of thumb that could be applied mechanically."[4]

and further explains that some of the conceptual uncertainties or obscurities are essentially caused by the need to satisfy most experts, home and abroad, about the form and content of a complicated statement to be used by a number of countries.

The analyst should not be intimidated. He does not have to get involved in the abstruse theological discussions of the experts. The basic principles governing the compilation and the interpretation of the information contained in the balance of payments are not as complicated as they may seem.

Notwithstanding its lack of precision, the balance of payments remains the principal source of information for any factual comparison of international re-

---

[3]Ibid., Chapter 7, Analytic Presentation, under (2) Common Types of Analytic Balance, p. 52.
[4]Ibid., Preface, p. XIII.

payment cpabilities. The analyst will have to get used to the idea that he is dealing with some concepts that are not entirely clear. He should also be constantly aware that he is dealing with approximations because all statistics are approximate. However, the individual statistical series of the balance of payments allow many interesting and informative comparisons among countries.

The *Manual* does not include a glossary; however a glossary was published in the February 5 and 19, 1979 issues of the "IMF Survey;" the text is reproduced in Appendix I for the convenience of the reader.

STATISTICAL ACCURACY

There are four basic elements that may affect the statistical accuracy of the balance of payments: the residence of the transacting parties, the valuation of the transaction, the timing, and the exchange rate applied.

The following comments are based on the rules outlined in the *Manual* for the compilation of the balance of payments.

Although the *Manual* specifies what *residents* are, the fact remains that the legal definition of residency varies among countries. As a result, the transactions of certain entities or individuals may be included by some countries in the balance of payments or may be excluded by other countries.

The basis for the *valuation* of any transaction is the market price, which is the price that a willing buyer pays to a willing seller when the buyer and seller are independent parties whose only considerations are commercial ones. Uncertainties arise when one or more of the conditions needed to establish a market price are absent.

Timing on the whole is an easier concept to deal with than valuation, although it is by no means without statistical problems that can have a significant impact on the figures to be recorded. The basic principle is that transactions are to be recorded when the real resources or financial items involved undergo a legal change of ownership. By convention, the time of change of ownership is normally taken to be the time when the parties concerned record the transactions on their books, which is not necessarily the same time for all the parties involved.

As to the *exchange rate*, the theory is that the conversion from transaction currencies to the national currency should be made in such a way as to reflect their relationship at the time when the contract was entered into. In practice, however, the contracting parties frequently report the time of payment. Moreover, trade figures may be converted by customs officials in accordance with legislative prescription which may not reflect the actual market rates. Finally, the totals of the transactions in national currencies will have to be converted into an international common denominator such as Special Drawing Rights (SDRs); that is usually done on the basis of the average of the market rates during the period in which the transactions took place.

The analyst should consult the *Manual* for a more detailed discussion of the methods used and of the uncertainties involved in the compilation of the balance of payments.

PRESENTATION OF THE BALANCE OF PAYMENTS ACCOUNTS

Some readers may find it baffling that the *Balance of Payments Statistics* (BPS), published by the IMF, presents two versions of the balance of payments:

Table 1—Aggregate Presentation

Table 2—Detailed Presentation

The Aggregate Presentation is basically a summary of the data of the Detailed Presentation, classified into groups that are considered relevant by the Fund's staff for analyzing the international economic relationships of the reporting countries in a uniform manner. As the name indicates, the "Detailed Presentation" gives a more detailed picture of the external accounts.

Of the two presentations, the Detailed Presentation is much more useful for country creditworthiness evaluation purposes than the Aggregate Presentation. Each presentation is discussed below.

Aggregate Presentation

The accounts are subdivided into eight groups:

A. Current Account, excluding Group F
B. Direct Investments and Other Long-Term Capital, excluding Groups F through II
C. Other Short-Term Capital, excluding Groups F through H
D. Net Errors and Omissions
E. Counterpart Items
F. Exceptional Financing
G. Liabilities Constituting Foreign Authorities Reserves
H. Total Change in Reserves.

Although the Aggregate Presentation is a summary of the Detailed Presentation, the two presentations do not follow the same principles in grouping various items. The reader will find a key to the reconciliation of the two presentations on page VI of Vol. 31 of the BPS. A listing of the items included in the Aggregate Presentation will be found on the same page, while a listing of the items of the Detailed Presentation is found on page XVII.

The Aggregate Presentation should be examined for creditworthiness evaluation clues because it is the presentation used in the monthly supplements of the BPS.

The Current Account section lists credit and debit of "merchandise" and credit and debit of "other goods, services, and income." Only the imbalance is reported for "private unrequited transfers" and "official unrequited transfers."

"Investment income," which includes debit interest due on external debt, is an optional entry reported separately for about one half of the countries: credit and debit of "investment income" are indicated only one or two times out of ten.[5]

Groups B, C, and H show the origin of the bulk of the funds needed to finance current account deficits, or other items. Groups E, F, and G are of secondary importance for creditworthiness evaluation.

The origin, for instance, of the increases of more than 100 percent in the reserves of three countries, mentioned at the beginning of this chapter, is shown by the following computation:

Years 1977 and 1978	Paraguay	Ghana	Costa Rica
Aggregate Presentation BPS		(million SDRs)	
B–Direct Investment and Other Long-Term Capital	206	164	538
C–Other Short-Term Capital	174	− 18	78
Groups E, F and G*	− 26	187	28
New External Liabilities	354	333	644
Current Account Deficit	140	105	483
Increase Reserves	209	143	97
N.E. & O.	5	85	64
	354	333	644
New External Liabilities as Percentage of Reserves Increase	169	233	664

*E–Counterpart Items; F–Exceptional Financing; G–Liabilities Constituting Foreign Authorities Reserves.
Source: *Balance of Payments Statistics*, Vol 32.

The calculations show that the big reserve increases of the three countries were not due to better performance of the external accounts but instead were due to new borrowing. As a fact, in each country new borrowing exceeded reserve increase by a good margin, in the case of Costa Rica by six to one.

[5]First 20 countries listed in Balance of Payments Statistics, Vol. 3.

Detailed Presentation

Although the Detailed Presentation is reported on a yearly basis, meaning that the data have a time lag of at least one year, the analyst is compelled, by lack of similar more up-to-date data, to rely on it for a basic external repayment capability evaluation (see Chapter 11, under "External Repayment Capability"). This situation will have to be accepted unless the IMF decides to rearrange the BPS monthly supplements toward a creditworthiness evaluation approach.

As stated at the beginning of this chapter, the Detailed Presentation, which consists of 112 items, is subdivided into four sections:

— Current Account
— Capital Account
— Reserves
— Net Errors and Omissions

The Current Account is the key to the assessment of a country's performance in the international field. The details are discussed in Chapter 14 CURRENT ACCOUNT, Chapter 15 GROSS EXTERNAL REVENUES (GER) and Chapter 16 FINANCIAL INCOME AND EXPENDITURES (Investment Income). The Capital Account is discussed below. Reserves are discussed in Chapter 6 LIQUIDITY PROBLEMS. Net Errors and Omissions are discussed in this chapter.

The notes at the end of the Detailed Presentation point out items whose composition is different from the concepts outlined in the *Manual*.

THE CAPITAL ACCOUNT

The Capital Account of the Detailed Presentation consists of the following sections:

— Direct Investments
— Portfolio Investments
— Long-term debt
— Short-term debt

The distinction between equity investments and debts is obviously important in the evaluation of the external position of a country. Fixed obligations have to be paid (or refinanced) when they become due, while equity investments can go on indefinitely. However, there is an additional important distinction to be made among equity investments: some are direct investments and some are portfolio investments. In the international field direct investments are much more important than portfolio investments. In most developing countries portfolio investments are relatively insignificant.

DIRECT INVESTMENTS AND PORTFOLIO INVESTMENTS

Direct investments are made to acquire a lasting interest in the enterprise operating in the country, with the purpose of having an effective voice in the management. As a result, the investor's association with the enterprise can be expected to continue for a considerable period of time. On the other hand, portfolio investors are primarily concerned about the safety of their capital, the return of the investment, and the possibility of its appreciation in value. Portfolio investors may shift their capital with changing conditions.

One may conclude that direct investments have an inherent element of stability, while, in contrast, portfolio investments are more volatile, and that is relevant to creditworthiness analysis. Direct investments are similar to capital contributions in a business enterprise.

As is the case with other balance of payments concepts, the distinction between direct investments and portfolio investments is not clear cut. As the overall proportion of the foreign ownership decreases or is dispersed among various owners, the distinction becomes increasingly difficult to establish. Many countries accept as evidence of direct investment the proportion of foreign ownership in the voting stock in the enterprise. However, the national practices vary among countries; hence, one cannot reasonably single out a percentage level as a well-founded standard that could be applied to all countries.

When foreign ownership is concentrated in the hands of one investor, or a group of associates, the percentage chosen as evidence of direct investments is typically quite low (frequently ranging from 25 percent down to 10 percent); apparently the tendency has been toward adopting percentages at the lower end of the range.

The analyst should, of course, be aware of the difficulty of defining precisely direct investments and of applying the concept in practice. However, the *Manual* points out that these problems do not necessarily have a corresponding importance for the validity and intercountry comparabiity of the statistics on direct investments. Most direct investment enterprises, in fact, either are branches or are subsidiaries that are wholly owned by foreigners or in which a clear majority of the voting stock is held by a single foreign investor or group. The real border line cases are thus likely to form a rather small proportion of the whole. Moreover, since the inconsistencies in classification occur mostly when the share of the foreign investor is quite small, the weight of the doubtful cases tends in principle to be further reduced by the rule that only the direct investor's share in the capital and income flows is to be classified as direct investment.

The details given for Direct Investments and Portfolio Investments vary greatly from country to country. Vol. 32 of the BPS, for instance, reports 18 items for Mexico's "portfolio investments," while one item is reported for Brazil.

LONG-TERM DEBT AND SHORT-TERM DEBT

According to balance of payments terminology both equity capital and fixed obligations (money borrowed or lent) are called capital. Equity capital is reported first in the balance of payments statistics as "Direct Investment" or "Portfolio Investment"; fixed obligations are called "Other Long-Term Capital" or "Other Short-Term Capital."

Long-term borrowing or lending is divided into three parts:

— Other long-term capital of resident official sector
— Other long-term capital of money banks sector
— Other long-term capital of other sectors.

Short-term borrowing or lending is also divided into three parts along the same lines.

The details given vary from country to country. Vol. 32 of the BPS, for instance, reports 54 items for Brazil's "Other Long-Term Capital of Resident Official Sector," while eight items are reported for Mexico.

The information listed under "Other Long-Term Capital" and "Other Short-Term Capital" may be useful to update and check the accuracy of data listed in the World Debt Tables of the World Bank and of other information required to compile the "External Debt Profile," which is discussed in Chapter 7.

VARIOUS KINDS OF BALANCES OF PAYMENTS

The data of the balance of payments statistics may be used to compile various kinds of balances of payments, going under various names. Examples are Overall Balance of Payments, which is also referred to as Official Settlements Balance of Payments, Basic Balance of Payments, Balance of Payments in Current Account, and so on.

As mentioned under "Terminology" at the beginning of this chapter, it is desirable to specify precisely the components of any balance of payments that is being used.

Most widely used until the mid 1970s was the Overall Balance of Payments. It includes all economic dealings of a country with the rest of the world, regardless of whether the positive flow of foreign exchange represents money *earned* abroad, or *borrowed* abroad, or the proceeds of equity investments acquired in the country by nonresidents. On the other side it reflects foreign exchange outflow regardless of whether it is due to external expenditures, repayments of external obligations, money lent abroad, or the acquisition of equity investments abroad.

The imbalance of all these transactions is ultimately reflected in increases or decreases of the official reserves and is therefore sometimes called the "Official Settlements Balance of Payments."

The wording "Overall Balance of Payments" conveys the impression that its imbalance indicates the difference between a country's external income and expenditures, and as such reflects the country's international performance. In fact it is only a cash flow presentation.

The overall balance of payments of the three countries, for instance, that doubled their reserves showed nice surplus in 1977 and 1978, while their performance was not good from a creditworthiness point of view (see "Aggregate Presentation" above).

The *Manual* reports that ". . . the United States decided in mid-1976 . . . to discontinue official publication of all balances of that kind (overall balance of payments); it was considered that these balances might be encouraging preconceived and perhaps misleading conclusions about the balance of payments . . ."[6].

The Basic Balance of Payments is a modified version of the overall balance of payments; its computation includes the current account, direct equity investments, and long-term credits.

On the other hand, the balance of payments in the current account is a performance indicator. It reflects the imbalance between external revenues and external expenditures. Furthermore, it shows whether, and to what extent, a country is accumulating new external liabilities. This will be discussed in Chapters 14, 15, and 16.

NET ERRORS AND OMISSION

The last entry in the Detailed Presentation is "Net Errors and Omissions" (N.E. & O.). The troublesome question that arises in the compilation of any balance of payments is how to deal with this residual item. The figure is needed to balance the books because in theory total credits should balance total debits.

Net Errors and Omissions is the result of inconsistencies in evaluation, timing and exchange rates in the estimates used, and errors in the compilation of the statement and of omissions from the statement. Since the origin of the residual imbalance is not known, one does not know what part of it should be applied to the current account or to the capital account.

Some analysts are inclined to believe that the statistics for the short-term movements of capital are less reliable and that the imbalance should be applied to short-term capital movements. However, the statistics required to compile the

[6]*Balance of Payments Manual.* Chapter 7, Analytic Presentation, (2) Common Types of Analytic Balance, p. 51.

current account often contribute importantly to net errors and omissions. This means that the balance of payments wil be probably inaccurate regardless of whether the N.E. & O. are included in the current or the capital account. It seems, therefore, advisable to indicate residual items separately, calculating two balances, one with the other without N.E. & O. The two figures will indicate the low and the high limits of the range in which the actual figure should fall.

One should keep in mind that some errors and omissions which occur in the compilation of the balance of payments will almost certainly offset one another; the size of the residual imbalance does not necessarily indicate the overall accuracy of the statement.

The *Manual* states that:

> "An empirical rule of thumb that is sometimes quoted holds that a residual is large enough to create a problem when it exceeds the equivalent of 5% of the gross credit and debit entries for merchandise combines (although the residual can also arise, of course, from nonmerchandise transactions)."[7]

A more logical way of measuring the inaccuracies of the balance of payments statistics is to relate them to the gross external revenues. That is the amount of foreign exchange earned that will be available for external payments. N.E. & O. gives an indication of how much foreign exchange may be missing, or may be available in excess of the amounts indicated by the accounts.

The following table gives an indication of the range of approximation of the balance of payments statistics. It shows "N.E. & O. as Percentage of the Gross External Revenues (GER)" of a sample of 60 countries for the five years 1973 to 1977.

N.E. & O. as percentage of GER	Number of Countries						
	1973	1974	1975	1976	1977	Total	Percent
1 or less	14	8	12	13	11	58	19%
2 or 3	31	36	27	28	27	149	50%
4 or 5	5	7	13	10	11	46	15%
from 6 to 10	8	6	5	5	9	33	11%
Over 10	2	3	3	4	2	14	5%
MEDIAN: 2%							

The overall accuracy seems to be only fair. When making comparisons among countries, the analyst will have to assume that there is an 80 percent probability

[7]Ibid., Chapter 8, Standard Components, (3) Net Errors and Omissions, p. 62.

of an error of at least one percent in the results, apart from possible compensating errors and omissions.

Notwithstanding all implied inconsistencies and inaccuracies of balance of payments data, and the explicit use of a "N.E. & O." item to balance the books, many analysts are in the habit of calculating ratios to the last decimal point. As Irving S. Friedman said "What mattered was the number of decimal points calculated for this (debt service) ratio. This approach still plagues our thinking. We grope for precision where there is no precision. . . ."[8] The preoccupation with meaningless precision is regrettable because it conveys the illusion of an accuracy which has no factual basis.

[8]Irving S. Friedman. *Assessing Country Risk*. Euromoney Publications, London, 1981; Introduction: The Evolution of Country Risk Assessment, p. 12.

chapter 14

Current Account

Conventional international lending theories are based on the assumption that the bulk of external borrowing is made for economic development purposes. The subject is discussed in Chapter 5, under GROWTH-CUM-DEBT THEORIES.

There is, of course, a sound basis for the theory that economic growth of developing countries is helped by external borrowing. Less sound, however, is the assumption that economic growth will be automatically accompanied by an increase of foreign exchange earnings.

At any rate, private bank lending during the 1970s was hardly growth connected; it consisted of a number of mostly unrelated loans used by the borrowers to obtain foreign exchange which they needed. That growth considerations were not involved is evident if one considers the short-term nature of the loans, mostly two or three years; during such short periods there is not enough time for economic growth theories to work.

What happened is that while economists were thinking in terms of "resources gaps," borrowers and lenders were filling everyday foreign exchange needs.

PRIVATE LENDER'S VIEWPOINT

It is advisable to rearrange international creditworthiness thinking by leaving growth-cum-debt theories to the World Bank and other official lenders.

In general, the purposes of a private lender's creditworthiness evaluation differ from those of the World Bank. The World Bank does not only lend money, it acts also as consultant and advisor to the borrowing countries and, sometimes, is the originator of new economic policies.

There are also practical reasons for a different approach. As Stephen D. Eccles of the World Bank states "We are dealing in number of economists per country, whereas commercial banks usually talk of the number of countries per economist . . ."[1]

Private lenders should concentrate their attention on the external repayment capability of the borrower; that means essentially a thorough examination of the balance of payments in the current account, or "current account" as it is commonly called.

The analyst should, above all, keep in mind that external debt cannot be repaid unless the current account shows a surplus. The country may draw temporarily on its international reserves and related assets, it may be able to attract new equity investments, but the overall repayment of external debts depends ultimately on a current account surplus.

The calculation is: current account imbalance plus or minus changes in foreign equity investments plus or minus changes in reserves equals increase or deccrease of external debt.

Foreign equity investments, one should point out, do not give a free ride since profits have to be remitted to foreign owners. Reserves, as monetary authorities well know, are a limited asset.

In the long run, the repayment of external debts depends on a country's ability to generate a current account surplus.

CONCEPTUAL BASIS

The concept on which the current account is based is simple enough. It follows broadly the principles that regulate the compilation of the profit and loss account of a business enterprise. One exception is that in the current account the acquisition of capital goods is considered as an expenditure; therefore, no provision is made for depreciation.

Money borrowed or lent abroad, the acquisition of external financial assets and external equity investments, and the acquisition or sale by nonresidents of financial assets and equities in the country are excluded from the current account because they cause corresponding liabilities or assets.

The surplus or deficit of the current account reflects the imbalance between foreign exchange revenues and expenditures.

One should note that the meaning of "current account" is not unequivocal.

---

[1]Stephen D. Eccles. "Financing and Risk in Developing Countries." In *Proceedings of a Symposium on Developing Countries' Debt*. Sponsored by the Export-Import Bank of the United States, August 1977; Chapter 15, Panel Discussion: Managing and Assessing Developing Country Risk, p. 105.

The IMF *Balance of Payments Manual*, for instance, refers to a ". . . version of the current account showing goods, services and income . . .[2], while the current account imbalance indicated in both the Detailed Presentation and the Aggregate Presentation of the *Balance of Payments Statistics* include goods, services, income, and unrequited transfers.

Some analysts include in the current account goods, services, and income and leave out unrequited transfers; others include private unrequited transfers, while others include both private and official unrequited transfers.

When using current account imbalance data, it is therefore essential to find out what is included in the figures reported.

The current account data reported in the Aggregate Presentation and the Detailed Presentation of the *Balance of Payments Statistics* are used for this study.

GROSS EXTERNAL REVENUES (GER)

The credit side of the current account includes amounts earned from merchandise exports, for the performance of services such as transportation and insurance for nonresidents, earnings from foreign tourism, interest earned on credits extended abroad, and dividends earned on investments made abroad as well as royalties, financial services rendered, earnings from building contracts abroad, and any other amount earned abroad; in other words, all external earnings of a country.

The credit side of the current account also includes some revenues which are not earned but which add to the international assets of a country without creating corresponding liabilities. They are called "unrequited transfers" and include remittances received from nationals working abroad, pensions received from foreign sources, private donations, and foreign government aid.

The total of all such external revenues is called in this book "Gross External Revenues" (GER) (see Chapter 15).

GROSS EXTERNAL EXPENDITURES (GEE)

On the debit side, one finds expenditures for goods imported and services received from residents of other countries, expenditures of nationals traveling abroad, debit interest paid or due on external borrowings, and the profits paid or due on foreign investments in the country as well as "unrequited transfers" such as monies sent abroad by foreigners working in the country, pensions sent abroad, private donations, and government aid to other countries.

---

[2]*Balance of Payments Manual*, Chapter 7, Analytic Presentation, (2) Common Types of Analytic Balance, p. 53.

"Reinvested earnings on direct investments in the country" are included on the debit side of the current account. They are future obligations and therefore are entered as expenditures the way accrued expenses are included in a business profit and loss account; in short, all expenditures and transfers abroad for which no credit is received. The total of all such external expenditures is called in this book "Gross External Expenditures" (GEE).

THE CURRENT ACCOUNT IMBALANCE

The imbalance of the current account is one of the most significant performance indicators for international creditworthiness analysis.

A surplus in the current account indicates that external revenues of the country are higher than its external expenditures, that the country is spending less than it is earning abroad, and that the country is accumulating assets abroad. Conversely, deficits in current account indicate that the country is overspending and as a result creating new external liabilities.

A surplus of external revenues over external expenditures is necessary in the long run for the repayment of external debts. The size of the recent current account deficits indicates how much of an increase in external revenues and/or decrease in external expenditures will be needed to balance the current account in order to stop the accumulation of new external liabilities and start the repayment of external debts.

Nothing is more important for the country creditworthiness analysis than to know the fundamental relationship between external revenues and external expenditures as reflected by the current account.

The information about the external revenues and expenditures of a country is either available in the current account or is not available at all. Any factual evaluation of the external repayment capabilities of a country has to be based on the information itemized in the current account.

USEFULNESS OF CURRENT ACCOUNT DATA FOR CREDITWORTHINESS EVALUATION

The usefulness of the information listed in the current account for international creditworthiness evaluation may be summarized as follows:

— it lists in detail all external revenues and expenditures;
— it indicates the imbalance between external revenues and expenditures, thus showing whether the country is spending abroad more than it is earning;

— it indicates the "gross external revenues" which should be used instead of the GNP/GDP for the computation of ratios related to the external accounts (see Chapter 15);

— it lists the information necessary for the computation of the ratio "Debit Interest on External Debts as Percentage of GER," the ratio "Imbalance Between External Debit and Credit Interest as Percentage of GER," and the ratio "Imbalance Between External Debit and Credit Interest Plus Imbalance Between Profits Due and Receivable on Foreign Equity Investments as Percentage of GER" (see Chapter 16, FINANCIAL INCOME AND EXPENDITURES);

— it reflects the results of a country's government economic policies in regard to its external accounts;

— the deficits of the current account (if any) indicate how much of the capital needed for the economic development of a country has to be borrowed abroad (see Chapter 5, under "The Resources Gap").

Incidentally, the fact that a country has sizeable current account deficits indicates that some lenders—official and/or private—consider it creditworthy. If the lenders refuse to come across with new money, and if foreign aid is not forthcoming, the country will have to tighten its belt, unless it has sizeable reserves. A country cannot run a series of substantial current account deficits if it cannot borrow the money to finance them. The analyst should keep in mind the possibility that smaller current account deficits may reflect mostly the fact that lenders are reluctant to extend new credit rather than, for instance, better export performance or less expansionary economic policies.

UNCERTAINTY ABOUT MEANING OF CURRENT ACCOUNT IMBALANCE

The main weakness—from the viewpoint of a sound creditworthiness evaluation—of current account data, as they are presented today, is mentioned at the beginning of this chapter under "Conceptual Basis." The current account does not separate outlays for capital goods from current expenditures for supplies, raw material, or consumption.

Details about the composition of imports are seldom given in the BPS and, if given, are not very illuminating. For example, some industrial countries list "gold" or "non-monetary gold" imports separately; some African developing countries list "smuggled goods" or "smuggled goods f.o.b." The "f.o.b." notation is interesting because it shows that some authorities may have a sense of humor.

In 1983 the IFS began publishing a *Supplement on Trade Statistics* which reports data on "manufactured goods" imports but does not differentiate between capital goods and consumer goods. Manufactured goods are not necessarily capital goods; they could be textiles, television sets, or power plant turbines, so that it is not possible to separate investments from consumption.

Another uncertainty is that the collectability of the amounts reported is not assured. Doubts about the prompt collectability of some foreign exchange earnings is not uncommon in industrial countries that sell capital goods on credit. But developing countries are not immune. Brazil, for instance, appears among Poland's creditors.

Some observers believe that current acount data should be adjusted for inflation. Jack Guenther, for instance, states that "We talk about adjusting bank accounting for inflation; we should actually consider a system of adjusting balance of payments data to take account of inflation. Such an adjustment, by removing the part of interest payments which reflects inflation, would sharply reduce the current account deficits of heavy debtor countries such as Brazil."[3] Guenther, of course, has a point.

As a result of inflation the debtor in effect pays part of the debt now, instead of paying when it becomes due; that means that in real terms the debt is reduced by the difference between the original value in real terms and the real value after currency devaluations due to inflation.

The problem is to determine the reduction of the debt in real terms. One may, for instance, simply take a country's external debt and reduce it by an inflation rate. But which rate? A country's "export unit values" index? "World commodity prices" indexes? Or, assuming that the debt is in dollars, the U.S. wholesale prices index?

As an alternative, one may take the "London Interbank Offer Rate (LIBOR) on U.S. Dollar Deposits" rate, add one or two percent for spread, and then deduct one of the above mentioned inflation rate indexes in order to calculate the interest rate in real terms.

Another problem is that a country's international assets, including "reserves minus gold," also depreciate with inflation, and their value should be adjusted. In any case, inflationary adjustments should be limited to interest payable and receivable because inflation will inflate other income and expenditures so that no adjustments are needed for the other items of the current account.

It would seem that since debts will be paid in nominal dollars (or other currency) one may just as well use data expressed in nominal currency for creditworthiness calculations.

Most observers believe that inflation invariably favors debtors, but that is not always the case; the ultimate benefit of inflation to debtors is unpredictable because it depends on the interplay between rates of inflation and nominal interest rates.

[3]Jack Guenther. *Assessing Country Risk*. Euromoney Publications, London, 1981; Chapter 20, The Outlook for the 1980s, p. 156.

THE TRADE BALANCE

One bothersome problem is the use of the term "trade balance." It derives from the habit of using the words "imports" and "exports" loosely, sometimes to describe merchandise transactions, other times to include merchandise and services—at times only factor services, other times including non-factor services, moreover, sometimes to include private unrequited transfers. (See also Chapter 5, under "Reserves to Imports Ratio.")

The use of the term "trade balance" should be avoided. One should always clearly specify what kind of balance is meant.

Invisibles—service, income, and unrequited transfers—should always be included in creditworthiness evaluations. To leave out invisibles is tantamount to leaving out services in a country's GDP calculation.

CURRENT ACCOUNT DATA TIME LAG

Although there is no doubt that invisibles should always be included in any creditworthiness evaluation, there is the problem of the time lag between the publication of merchandise trade statistics and the publication of the current account figures.

Checking the information published in the IFS one finds that the time lag between the merchandise export-import figures and those of the current account is not as bad as one would suspect. As an example, the time lags appearing in the December 1979 IFS issue are summarized in the following table.

Time Lag Between Merchandise Export-Import and Current Account
Statistics—December 1979 IFS

No time lag	31 countries	28%
Time lag 1 to 3 months	18 countries	16%
Time lag 4 to 6 months	25 countries	23%
Time lag 7 to 12 months	28 countries	25%
Time lag 12 months or more	9 countries	7%
Total 111 countries		

A time lag of six months or less for two thirds of the countries is really not bad.

However, some times it may be desirable to update the information given in the merchandise trade account by estimating the imbalance of invisible items for the lag period.

Several methods could be used for this purpose. The easiest one is to adjust the merchandise export/import imbalance of a certain period (quarterly, for instance) by adding or subtracting the imbalance shown by invisible items during the most recent corresponding period. This method may be criticized as being simplistic, but it works out reasonably well in practice since current account imbalance estimates usually cover periods shorter than 12 months.

CURRENT ACCOUNT IMBALANCE AS PERCENTAGE OF GER

The relative size of current account imbalances is no doubt one of the key elements for a country's creditworthiness evaluation because it gives an indication of how difficult it will be to balance the external accounts.

The current account imbalance is traditionally related to GDP, but, as pointed out under "GDP or GNP Denominators" in Chapter 5, the GER component in GDP varies from country to country, and since external obligations can be repaid only with foreign exchange, it is frequently misleading to relate a foreign exchange gap to GDP.

Current account deficits will, therefore, be related to gross external revenues in this book, as indicated in Chapter 11, under "External Repayment Capability."

As is the case with most variables or indicators, the "Current Account Deficit as Percentage of GER" ratio has its weak points of which the analyst should be aware.

In a number of countries part of the current account deficit is covered by funds coming in as direct investments. A good example is Mexico where in 1980 about 25 percent of the current account deficit was offset by direct investments.

Table 9 Current Account Imbalance as Percentage of Gross External Revenues (GER)—Averages 1978/1980—Averages 1979/1980—Year 1980

Relative Indicator*				
1978/1980	1979/1980	1980		1980 Ratio
28	Cred. 112	Cred. 169	Venezuela	Cred. 18.9
Cred. 47	Cred. 96	Cred. 117	Indonesia	Cred. 12.9
Cred. 133	Cred. 135	Cred. 107	So. Africa	Cred. 11.9
Cred. 87	Cred. 75	Cred. 89	Malta	Cred. 10.0
Cred. 10	Cred. 9	Cred. 33	United Kingdom	Cred. 3.6
33	2	Cred. 31	Norway	Cred. 3.5
10	Cred. 7	Cred. 10	United States	Cred. 1.1
Cred. 54	Cred. 42	5	Colombia	.4
Cred. 54	Cred. 23	12	Switzerland	1.3
51	37	19	Canada	2.1
26	26	26	Netherlands	2.8

(continued)

Table 9 *(Continued)*

*Relative Indicator**				1980 Ratio
1978/1980	*1979/1980*	*1980*		
Cred. 21	Cred. 23	29	Malaysia	3.2
5	19	41	France	4.6
138	121	48	Egypt	5.3
19	45	58	Germany	6.5
45	52	58	Belgium	6.5
26	44	60	Iceland	6.6
96	86	60	Israel	6.7
3	65	62	Japan	6.8
23	49	72	Finland	8.0
126	96	74	Guatemala	8.3
Cred. 5	21	81	Italy	8.9
135	93	83	Tunisia	9.2
100	100	95	New Zealand	10.5
296	224	95	Bolivia	10.6
89	105	100	Jamaica	11.1
112	126	108	Ireland	12.0
89	93	108	Austria	12.1
14	44	114	Spain	12.7
82	103	122	Sweden	13.5
201	187	132	Pakistan	14.8
98	65	136	Syria	15.1
176	138	143	Australia	15.9
264	208	175	Ecuador	19.4
215	203	189	Cyprus	21.1
173	208	206	So. Korea	23.0
203	213	210	Greece	23.3
241	231	222	Philippines	24.6
271	273	239	Thailand	26.5
290	255	258	Chile	28.6
308	299	267	Mexico	29.7
383	338	280	Morocco	31.1
248	261	292	Honduras	32.4
159	108	320	Zambia	35.5
336	355	361	Paraguay	40.2
234	282	366	Sri Lanka	40.6
322	315	390	Turkey	43.3
383	408	409	Kenya	45.3
462	486	470	Costa Rica	52.2
542	534	490	Brazil	54.6
539	488	576	Tanzania	63.9

*100 equals median ratio of countries listed; i.e., 9.9% for 1978/1980, 10.4% for 1979/1980, and 11.1% for 1980.

Source: *Balance of Payments Statistics*, Vol. 32.

Such investments should be deducted from the current account deficit in order to estimate new borrowing which will create new debt servicing burdens.

In the long run, however, direct investments also require foreign exchange servicing, so that, all considered, the "Current Account Imbalance as Percentage of GER" ratio is a good indicator of the additional burdens which will weigh in the future on a country's foreign exchange earnings.

Table 9 reports "Current Account Imbalances as Percentage of GER" for 51 countries for the years 1978 to 1980.

The first three columns report relative indicators—in which 100 equals the median of the countries listed—for the periods 1978/80, 1979/80, and 1980. The fourth column reports 1980 ratios. The countries are listed on the basis of increasing 1980 ratios.

CURRENT ACCOUNT IMBALANCE AS PERCENTAGE OF GER INCREASE

The ratio does not seem to be commonly used for creditworthiness evaluations; most analysts relate current account deficits to GDP or GDP increases.

Some observers, however, are aware of the importance of relating current account deficits to foreign exchange revenue increases. Morgan Guaranty, for instance, published in June, 1983 a table "Growth of total external debt and exports for 21 major LDC borrowers," which compares per annum percent debt increases with "exports of goods, services and private transfers" percent increases[4].

Rapidly expanding GER means that more foreign exchange will be available for the repayment of external obligations, while stagnating foreign exchange earnings will leave no margin for new burdens created by current account deficits.

One could theorize that, even if the current account were in deficit for substantial amounts, there could be a sufficiently rapid expansion of GER so that enough foreign exchange would become available for new servicing requirements and for inevitable external expenditure increases.

The problem is that loans are contracted for different lengths of time and at different rates of interest, so that servicing requirements will be different.

To obtain terms of comparison, one could simplify matters by assuming, for instance, that new loans will be repaid in equal yearly installments. On that basis, the following short table reflects various servicing requirements for the first year for loans of various duration at different interest rates:

Duration of loan (years)	3	5	10	20
Interest rate (percent)	20	15	10	5
Amortization rate (percent)	33	20	10	5
Total servicing (percent)	53	35	20	10

[4]*World Financial Markets.* Morgan Guaranty Trust Co. June 1983, p. 3.

To draw a general line below which GER increases, compared to current account deficits, would be deemed insufficient to cover new servicing requirements would be arbitrary. New external debt servicing requirements will inevitably compete for foreign exchange with increasing imports, and one may only guess about future government policies.

How significant is the "current account imbalance as percentage of GER increase" ratio?

On the basis of data used for the Brazil-Denmark "current account imbalance as percentage of GER" comparison, reported in Chapter 5 under "GDP or GNP Denominators," one finds that:

1978–1980	Brazil	Denmark
Deficit as percentage of		
GDP increase	56%	47%
GER increase	366%	100%

Source: *IFS* December 1981; *BPS*, Vol. 32.

The ratios based on GDP increases are not far apart for the two countries; but the foreign exchange revenue increases related ratios show that, on a relative basis, Brazil's debts were expanding more than three times faster than Denmark's.

Table 10 reports "Current Account Imbalances as Percentage of GER Increases" for 51 countries for the years 1978 to 1980. The table follows the outline of Table 9.

Table 10 Current Account Imbalance as Percentage of Gross External Revenues (GER) Increase—Averages 1978/1980—Averages 1979/1980—Year 1980.

*Relative Indicator**							*1980 Ratio*	
1978/1980		*1979/1980*		*1980*				
	29	Cred.	67	Cred.	83	Venezuela	Cred.	71
Cred.	70	Cred.	65	Cred.	60	Malta	Cred.	52
Cred.	32	Cred.	57	Cred.	51	Indonesia	Cred.	44
Cred.	78	Cred.	84	Cred.	48	So. Africa	Cred.	41
Cred.	8	Cred.	8	Cred.	22	United Kingdom	Cred.	19
	25		0	Cred.	17	Norway	Cred.	15
	10	Cred.	6	Cred.	8	United States	Cred.	7
Cred.	64	Cred.	57		3	Colombia		3
	62		48		16	Canada		14
Cred.	63	Cred.	41		17	Switzerland		15
	25		27		22	Netherlands		19
	110		98		22	Egypt		19

(continued)

Table 10   (*Continued*)

Relative Indicator*					1980 Ratio
1978/1980		1979/1980		1980	
Cred.	15	Cred.	17	26	Malaysia	22
	5		21	36	France	31
	3		78	40	Japan	34
	18		40	45	Finland	39
	37		48	48	Belgium	41
	100		95	49	Israel	42
	121		135	67	Pakistan	58
	22		62	69	Germany	59
	29		56	69	Iceland	59
	99		100	70	New Zealand	60
	353		227	70	Bolivia	60
	89		68	76	Tunisia	65
	296		146	78	Guatemala	67
	141		159	100	Mexico	86
	84		190	101	Jamaica	87
Cred.	5		24	107	Italy	92
	78		98	112	Austria	95
	182		135	126	Australia	108
	11		44	128	Spain	110
	196		192	137	Philippines	118
	196		214	147	Thailand	126
	174		159	156	Chile	134
	189		178	156	Cyprus	135
	237		170	160	Ecuador	138
	89		117	164	Sweden	141
	101		170	184	Ireland	158
	178		313	210	So. Korea	181
	114		48	220	Syria	189
	356		327	241	Morocco	207
	301		287	253	Turkey	218
	932		617	267	Kenya	230
	501		446	289	Brazil	249
	221		271	317	Sri Lanka	273
	360		427	350	Paraguay	301
	303		348	415	Honduras	357
	230		279	469	Greece	403
	1,627		1,235	787	Costa Rica	677
	295		138	Negative	Zambia	Negative
Negative		Negative		Negative	Tanzania	Negative

*100 equals median ratio of countries listed; i.e., 73 for 1978/1980, 63 for 1979/1980, and 86 for 1980.

Source: *Balance of Payments Statistics*, Vol. 32.

chapter 15

Gross External Revenues (GER)

Generating foreign exchange, whether by exporting goods or rendering services abroad, is a difficult and complicated business. First, the goods must be produced; second, the goods must be of acceptable quality and priced competitively; third, a market must be found for the goods. The same requirements apply to services rendered abroad.

It takes time, effort, and knowledge to build a successful export business. On the other hand, one may assume that a country which has a sound structural export capability will export successfully. The corollary is that past performance is the best indicator of a country's foreign exchange earning capability.

Most economists emphasize the price factor, namely, the level of foreign exchange rates, which may hinder or help exports, but other factors are equally if not more important.

The assumption that a government can promote exports is only partly valid. If, for instance, the authorities have set unrealistic foreign exchange rates, or have created export impediments, then one may say that their removal will help exports, provided the capacity to produce acceptable goods is there and there is a market for them.

FACTORS WHICH INFLUENCE FOREIGN EXCHANGE EARNINGS

Gross external revenues indicate a country's foreign exchange generating capability, which is the key to the repayment of its external obligations.

GER rising at a good rate indicates that a country is competitive on international markets. The comparison over time of the external revenues of a country with those of other countries, indicates whether the country is gaining or losing ground in international competition.

In brief, the size of the GER, its trends, and its past stability are more indicative of a country's external repayment potential than any other data.

The analyst should focus his attention on the following points:

— composition of GER
— trend over time of GER total
— stability of GER
— vulnerability of GER, due to concentration of foreign exchange earnings.

COMPOSITION OF GER

As mentioned in Chapter 14, under "Gross External Revenues," all credit items of the current account, as reported in the *Balance of Payments Statistics* published by the IMF, are included in GER. That means: goods exported, services rendered abroad, foreign income, private unrequited transfers, and official unrequited transfers.

Most observers exclude from the current account official unrequited transfers; such transfers nevertheless represent external revenues for the recipient and are therefore included, for the purposes of this study, in the GER calculation.

Some analysts seem to be under the impression that the earnings derived from exports of goods are the ones that really count; that non-merchandise earnings are relevant only in a few countries and, therefore, should be considered of secondary importance. That is not the case. Non-merchandise earnings are discussed separately in the following section.

"INVISIBLE" EXTERNAL EARNINGS

The term "invisibles," which was widely used in the past, has apparently gone out of fashion. Its meaning, however, is broad enough and clear enouh to designate all nonmerchandise external earnings and will be used for verbal convenience in this book to designate nonmerchandise external revenues.

The importance of invisible external earnings should not be underestimated. In 1980, for instance, they represented 28.6 percent of global international income, up from 26.9 percent of 1974. In SDR terms total invisibles went from 213 billion in 1974 to 515 billion in 1980, with an 142 percent increase[1].

[1]*Balance of Payments Statistics*, Vol. 32, Part 2, p. 40.

One may theorize that the share of invisible earnings in global trade will increase as the economies of most countries continue to evolve. A similar process is taking place in domestic economies, where the share of the service sector in the GDP/GNP increases as the economy evolves.

The share of GER represented by invisible earnings in a sample of 51 countries in 1980 is shown in Table 11.

The share of invisible earnings in gross external revenues varies from a high of 59 percent for Egypt and Malta to a low of 2 percent for Indonesia.

Observers who are under the impression that invisibles are important only for countries with substantial tourist trade or workers' remittances, may be surprised to see that 35 percent of 1980 foreign exchange revenues was represented by invisibles in the United States, the United Kingdom, and France (the three

Table 11   Invisibles* as Percentage of Gross External Revenues (GER) Year 1980

Egypt	59	Italy	30
Malta	59	Colombia	28
Cyprus	58	So. Korea	26
Greece	57	Thailand	25
Israel	56	Chile	24
Pakistan	56	Germany	24
Turkey	54	Iceland	24
Syria	50	Ireland	24
Tunisia	48	Guatemala	22
Morocco	46	Sweden	21
Austria	43	Japan	20
Kenya	43	Australia	19
Paraguay	43	Finland	19
Spain	43	New Zealand	18
Belgium	39	Costa Rica	18
Jamaica	39	Bolivia	16
Tanzania	39	Canada	16
France	35	Honduras	16
Mexico	35	Brazil	15
Sri Lanka	35	Ecuador	15
United Kingdom	35	So. Africa	14
United States	35	Venezuela	14
Norway	34	Malaysia	11
Switzerland	33	Zambia	11
Netherlands	32	Indonesia	2
Philippines	30		

*Non-merchandise foreign exchange revenues.
Source: *Balance of Payments Statistics*, Vol. 32.

countries combined earned more than one third of the more than 500 billion SDRs global 1980 invisible external revenues).

Industrial countries dominate the field because invisibles include banking, insurance, shipping, air transportation, foreign building contracts, and moreover income from foreign investments.

Analysts paying attention to "trade balances" reported by news media—normally reflecting only merchandise exports and imports—run the risk of getting a distorted picture of a country's external earnings. Invisibles should be included in all creditworthiness computations. If only merchandise export/import data are available, the amount of invisibles should be estimated (see Chapter 14, under "Current Account Data Time Lag").

Some aspects of invisible earnings are discussed under: "Workers' Remittances," "Tourist Earnings," and "Government Aid."

GER PERFORMANCE OVER TIME

To determine the performance of GER over time seems to be a straightforward problem. In practice, however, price inflation raises several difficulties.

An increase, for instance, of 13 percent in Spain's GER in 1980, or 11 percent in Sweden's GER, in SDR terms, seems quite satisfactory. But due to international prices inflation, the median increase of GER of a sample of 51

Table 12   Gross External Revenues (GER) Percentage Increase 1978/1980—1979/1980—1980

Relative Indicator*				Percent Increase**
1978/1980	1979/1980	1980		
235	212	312	Mexico	53
142	179	247	Indonesia	42
169	167	241	So. Africa	41
116	119	224	Egypt	38
151	195	212	Venezuela	36
169	138	206	Pakistan	35
124	126	182	Norway	31
100	117	171	Brazil	29
175	190	159	Chile	27
134	126	159	Thailand	27
118	124	153	Finland	26
118	117	153	Philippines	26
98	102	147	Turkey	25
118	114	141	Malta	24
84	74	141	Japan	24

(continued)

Table 12 (*Continued*)

Relative Indicator*				Percent Increase**
1978/1980	1979/1980	1980		
36	57	141	Kenya	24
130	121	135	United Kingdom	23
92	90	124	New Zealand	21
74	98	124	Bolivia	21
118	110	112	Belgium	19
88	81	112	Israel	19
114	107	106	United States	18
106	112	106	Cyprus	18
100	93	106	Morocco	18
160	155	100	Tunisia	17
146	143	100	Malaysia	17
116	95	100	France	17
98	100	100	Sri Lanka	17
96	95	100	Netherlands	17
90	100	100	Australia	17
74	79	100	Canada	17
106	126	94	Ecuador	16
112	90	88	Austria	15
94	60	88	So. Korea	15
84	76	88	Paraguay	15
54	48	88	Jamaica	15
76	67	82	Colombia	14
34	57	82	Guatemala	14
124	100	76	Spain	13
90	69	76	Iceland	13
86	67	71	Germany	12
106	88	65	Italy	11
88	86	65	Sweden	11
78	67	59	Honduras	10
104	171	53	Syria	9
86	45	53	Switzerland	9
110	71	47	Ireland	8
24	31	47	Costa Rica	8
84	74	35	Greece	6
76	114	Negative	Zambia	Negative
Negative	Negative	Negative	Tanzania	Negative

*100 equals median increase of the countries listed; i.e., 16.7% for 1978/1980, 21.0% for 1979/1980, and 17.0% for 1980.
**In SDR terms.

Source: *Balance of Payments Statistics*, Vol. 32.

countries in 1980 was 17 percent, meaning that GER increases of both countries were definitely below par.

To recompute foreign exchange earnings in real terms would be a lengthy and complicated process and the results would not be unequivocal. The relative performance of a country's GER may be determined without recomputing external revenues in real terms, by using relative indicators in which, for instance, the median GER increase of a group of countries represents one hundred.

Table 12 shows the 1980 GER percentage increase of 51 countries (last column). The other columns show relative indicators (median of sample equals 100) for 1978/80, 1979/80 and 1980.

The third column shows that in 1980 Spain's GER increase was 76 percent of the median, while Sweden's was 65 percent of the median of the countries listed.

GER INSTABILITY INDEX

Healthy GER increases are, of course, a good sign. But how resilient is a country's foreign exchange generating capability? How did external earnings stand up during past global recessions or during periods of government mismanagement?

The problem may be approached from two points of view:

1. Measure the stability, or instability, of foreign exchange earnings during past periods of adversity, and
2. look at their composition in order to estimate their vulnerability to exogeneous developments (discussed under "GER Concentration Index").

Several methods could be used to measure relative instability or stability of external earnings in order to compute what may be called a "gross external revenues instability index."

One simple procedure is to calculate the compounded average increase (or decrease) of gross external revenues during the base period; the difference between actual and average yearly increases (or decreases) represents the deviation from the basic trend. The average deviation is the instability index. For instance, if a country's compounded average GER increase during a base period was 6 percent, and if during a given year GER increased by 4 percent, there would be a 2 percent deviation for that year. The average of the yearly deviations would be the instability index.

Selection of the period to be used as a basis for the computations presents a difficult dilemma. The period should be sufficiently long to include two slowdowns in international trade. Practically this means ten years. The problem is that if one were to attempt to use the instability index for a five–year forecast, one would have a total time span of 15 years during which enormous changes could take place.

The long ten–year base period obviously weakens the present-day reliability of an instability index; however, a shorter period may reflect only fair weather performance. An index showing satisfactory GER stability does not imply that a country's external earnings are performing well, it only means that its foreign exchange earnings are steady. The stability may actually reflect stagnating GER. That weakness of the instability index should be kept in mind.

On average, countries with lower instability indexes should suffer less during periods of adversity than countries with higher instability index.

Table 13 reports the "Gross External Revenues Instability Index" for 51 countries for the ten–year 1971 to 1980 period.

Table 13   Gross External Revenues (GER) Instability Index—1971–1980

	Index	Relative Indicator*		Index	Relative Indicator*
France	3.9	42	Costa Rica	9.3	101
Austria	4.8	52	Brazil	9.7	105
Switzerland	5.1	55	Jamaica	9.9	108
Spain	5.3	58	Pakistan	10.2	111
Italy	5.4	59	So. Africa	10.8	117
Ireland	5.5	60	Cyprus	11.5	125
Greece	5.6	61	Morocco	11.5	125
Malta	5.6	61	Guatemala	11.9	129
Germany	6.1	66	Sri Lanka	11.9	129
United Kingdom	6.3	68	Kenya	12.2	133
Colombia	6.5	71	Turkey	12.5	136
Tanzania	6.9	75	Mexico	12.6	137
Australia	7.4	80	Paraguay	12.8	139
Netherlands	7.6	83	Tunisia	13.2	143
Canada	7.9	86	Egypt	15.1	164
Sweden	7.9	86	So. Korea	16.0	174
Norway	8.3	90	Bolivia	16.5	179
Finland	8.5	92	Malaysia	18.8	204
Iceland	8.5	92	Syria	23.3	253
Honduras	8.6	93	Ecuador	24.7	268
Belgium	8.8	96	Indonesia	25.0	271
Israel	8.8	96	Chile	25.3	275
New Zealand	8.9	97	Zambia	26.0	283
Japan	9.0	98	Philippines	27.5	299
Thailand	9.1	99	Venezuela	29.4	320
United States	9.2	100			

*100 equals median instability index of countries listed; i.e., 9.2.

Source: Various issues of *Balance of Payments Statistics*.

As could be expected, less developed countries (LDCs), with higher export concentration in a few commodities, have high GER instability indexes, while industrialized countries have lower ones.

No industrial country is included in the quartile with the higher instability indexes. Of the developing countries in the better quartile, Tanzania's low instability index reflects stagnation of foreign exchange earnings; on the other hand, Greece and Malta had good instability indexes and average GER increases during the ten–year period.

As to the relative performance of merchandise exports and invisible earnings, two questions arise:

1. How stable are merchandise exports?
2. Is external invisible income less stable than income derived from the sale of goods abroad, as some analysts seem to be inclined to believe?

Table 14 Merchandise Exports Instability Index—1971–1980.

	Index		Index
Ireland	3.0	Greece	11.0
France	4.9	Malta	12.4
Italy	6.0	Thailand	13.0
Spain	6.0	Guatemala	14.2
Switzerland	6.2	Kenya	14.5
Israel	6.7	Pakistan	14.5
Colombia	7.2	Turkey	14.8
Germany	7.2	Paraguay	15.3
Canada	7.5	Mexico	17.0
Sweden	7.5	Philippines	17.2
United Kingdom	7.7	Cyprus	17.4
Belgium	7.8	Jamaica	17.4
Australia	8.0	So. Africa	18.9
Norway	8.1	Morocco	19.6
Austria	8.3	So. Korea	20.7
Honduras	8.3	Malaysia	20.9
Netherlands	8.6	Egypt	22.1
Tanzania	9.5	Bolivia	22.3
Iceland	9.8	Syria	24.0
Brazil	9.9	Indonesia	24.5
Costa Rica	10.1	Tunisia	25.5
Finland	10.1	Chile	26.8
Japan	10.2	Ecuador	26.9
New Zealand	10.3	Zambia	28.0
Sri Lanka	10.6	Venezuela	31.0
United States	10.7		

Sources: Various issues of *Balance of Payments Statistics*.

The questions are answered by the following tables:

Table 14—Merchandise Exports Instability Index, 1971/1980.

Table 15—Invisible External Revenues Instability Index, 1971/1980.

The tables show a median instability index of 10.7 for merchandise exports and a median instability index of 11.0 for invisible external earnings. The difference is too small to be considered significant. The instability indexes of 51 countries over a period of ten years do not confirm the assumption that earnings derived from invisibles are inherently less stable than earnings derived from merchandise exports.

Some invisible external revenues which may seem particularly vulnerable to exogenous conditions are discussed under "Workers' Remittances," "Tourist Earnings," and "Government Aid."

Table 15   Invisible External Earnings Instability Index—1971–1980.

	Index		*Index*
Austria	3.5	Canada	11.3
Switzerland	3.7	Israel	11.8
Finland	3.8	Brazil	12.0
Morocco	4.5	Ireland	12.2
Germany	5.0	Belgium	13.1
France	5.2	Honduras	13.2
Greece	6.2	Colombia	13.4
Italy	7.0	Pakistan	13.4
Costa Rica	7.7	Malaysia	13.6
Jamaica	7.7	Zambia	13.6
Iceland	7.9	So. Africa	14.2
United States	8.0	Egypt	16.2
Tunisia	8.2	Kenya	16.7
Japan	8.3	Thailand	16.9
Australia	8.5	Turkey	19.2
Netherlands	8.5	Ecuador	21.1
Norway	8.6	Sri Lanka	21.3
Sweden	8.9	Paraguay	22.1
Malta	9.0	Indonesia	22.2
Spain	9.0	Guatemala	23.4
Bolivia	9.8	Venezuela	24.7
Philippines	10.0	So. Korea	24.8
Cyprus	10.2	Tanzania	25.7
Mexico	10.8	Chile	28.7
New Zealand	10.9	Syria	43.6
United Kingdom	11.0		

Sources: Various issues of *Balance of Payments Statistics*.

GER CONCENTRATION INDEX

There is no doubt that any concentration of external earnings in one or more commodities or services adds another element of uncertainty to the evaluation of the external creditworthiness of a country. To the extent of the concentration, the foreign exchange generating capability of a country depends on global demand and supply of the commodities and services sold. When commodities are involved, the external earnings are subject to boom and bust cycles of commodity markets.

What could be done to assess the additional risk caused by a specific concentration of external earnings?

First, one should point out that traditional concentration assessment takes into account commodities but ignores invisible earnings. That, of course, is erroneous; the computation should include invisibles and any product (for instance, ships, automobiles, or aircraft) or services that exceed a certain percentage (say 5) of GER.

Various methods are used to measure concentration. They consist mostly of determining the number of commodities accounting for a certain percentage, for instance, 40 or 60 percent of exports. The problem with this approach is that it does not take into consideration the relative size of each commodity (or service) concentration.

If four commodities (and/or services) were taken into account for a 60 percent total concentration, one could hypothesize, for instance, the following permutations adding up to 60 percent:

Country	(1)	(2)	(3)
1st commodity	20%	40%	57%
2nd commodity	15%	10%	1%
3rd commodity	15%	5%	1%
4th commodity	10%	5%	1%

In each case there are four commodities (or services) representing 60 percent of external revenues. The underlying situation is completely different however, with the highest commodity concentration going from 20 to 57 percent.

The problem of comparing different degrees of concentration may be overcome by using the Herfindahl index, which is calculated by squaring the share of each commodity or service concentration[2].

---

[2]*The Economist* (London), p. 72, reported on June 19, 1982, that the U.S. Justice Department intends to use this formula to determine market shares when considering approval of proposed mergers of large corporations.

The "sum of squares" concentration indexes for the above mentioned examples are:

country (1) 950, country (2) 1,750, country (3) 3,252. That gives a much clearer picture of the comparative situation of the three countries.

The Economist reported that "When the index is less than 1,000 the market is deemed unconcentrated (by the Justice Department) and mergers are 'unlikely' to be challenged. Between 1,000 and 1,800 on the index the market is moderately concentrated and over 1,800 highly so."[3]

If these standards were accepted, the first country's GER composition would be considered as unconcentrated, the second moderately concentrated, and the third highly concentrated. That is a big improvement in classification over a simple "number of commodities in 60 percent" ratio.

The "sum of squares" approach does not, however, solve the problem of reflecting the risk of what may actually happen: What are the probabilities that prices and demand of several commodities may decline at the same time? What would be the degree of decline in prices and demand for each commodity?

The "sum of squares" index gives a better idea of the vulnerability of GER;

Table 16 Sum of Squares GER Concentration Index—1978/1980, 1979/1980, and 1980.

Relative Indicator*				1980 Index**
1978/1980	1979/1980	1980		
0	0	0	Belgium	0
0	0	0	Germany	0
0	0	0	Japan	0
0	0	0	Netherlands	0
0	0	0	South Korea	0
0	0	0	United States	0
5	5	5	France	25
11	12	11	Italy	64
11	12	11	United Kingdom	64
13	14	12	Switzerland	81
16	16	12	Ireland	81
21	24	22	Sweden	138
36	38	33	Canada	210
44	42	36	Brazil	230
48	47	39	Australia	248

(*continued*)

[3]Ibid., p. 73.

Table 16 (*Continued*)

Relative Indicator*				1980 Index**
1978/1980	1979/1980	1980		
54	54	39	Philippines	250
57	59	50	Norway	314
64	66	56	Thailand	354
66	72	56	New Zealand	358
77	73	62	Spain	397
66	65	66	Israel	413
105	96	69	Tanzania	431
66	73	70	Cyprus	444
82	86	76	Austria	484
97	100	86	Greece	545
100	112	100	Finland	625
157	154	103	Costa Rica	653
146	128	105	Guatemala	655
85	110	115	Malta	725
120	96	123	Kenya	773
156	154	126	Paraguay	796
190	159	129	Sri Lanka	819
143	157	144	Malaysia	909
167	173	151	Morocco	954
194	205	158	Egypt	990
189	191	161	Honduras	1,015
166	203	177	Turkey	1,106
175	199	194	Tunisia	1,210
213	227	194	Iceland	1,213
241	241	201	Chile	1,254
241	245	222	Pakistan	1,388
223	238	250	Jamaica	1,566
356	334	267	Bolivia	1,667
348	336	302	Colombia	1,885
221	275	304	South Africa	1,961
243	299	339	Mexico	2,122
385	441	364	Syria	2,273
315	394	381	Ecuador	2,384
580	590	552	Indonesia	3,453
1,074	1,153	973	Venezuela	6,084
992	1,099	1,054	Zambia	6,586

*100 equals median concentration index of countries listed; i.e., 610 for 1978/1980, 570 for 1979/1980, and 625 for 1980.
**Sum of squares of each concentration of goods or services
Source: *Balance of Payments Statistics*, Vol. 32, *IFS*, December 1981.

it is, however, only a better approximation of potential risks caused by various degrees of concentration of external earnings.

One advantage of the "sum of squares" GER concentration index is that it is comparable regardless of the number of commodity concentrations in various countries.

Table 16 lists "sum of squares" concentration indicators for 1978/1980, 1979/1980, and 1980 for 51 countries. As in previous tables, the first three columns report indicators in which 100 equals the median of the countries listed. The last column reports the actual sum of the squares of commodities (or services) concentrations of each country in 1980. The table shows concentrations amounting to more than five percent of GER of items listed in the *BPS*,[4] or in the *IFS*[5] in any of the years 1978 to 1980.

WORKER'S REMITTANCES

The *Balance of Payments Statistics* does not indicate the world total for workers' remittances.[6] The seven countries mentioned below included in the standard 51 country sample—show a combined increase, in SDR terms of 172 percent from 1974 to 1980 against a 142 percent global increase of invisible earnings.

More recent entrants in the field, Pakistan, Egypt, and Morocco, show above average gains; Tunisia kept its share, while Spain, Greece, and Turkey lost some.

Workers' remittances would seem particularly vulnerable to unfavorable global economic conditions. One should logically assume that foreign workers would be the first ones to be dismissed and sent home when economic conditions get tight, and workers' remittances would drop dramatically. However, the experience during the 1974/1976 slowdown confirms this assumption only partially. Workers' remittances in Morocco and Tunisia increased faster than their GER, while Turkey and Greece lost ground.

It would seem that in an affluent society the nationals of the host country would rather collect unemployment benefits than do the humble work for which the guest workers were hired in the first place.

TOURIST EARNINGS (TRAVEL)

The *Balance of Payments Statistics*[7] reports an increase of global external "travel" income from 30.3 billion SDRs in 1974 to 75 billion SDRs in 1980, equal to 148 percent.

---

[4]*Balance of Payments Statistics*, Vol. 32.
[5]International *Financial Statistics*, December 1981.
[6]BPS, Vol. 32.
[7]Ibid.

The list of countries in which external tourist earnings represent five percent or more of GER is surprisingly long, 20 out of the 51 countries included in the standard sample. They are listed below, with the 1980 percentage of GER represented by travel income:

Austria	22	Malta	9
Colombia	6	Mexico	21
Cyprus	17	Morocco	10
Egypt	8	Paraguay	13
France	5	Spain	19
Greece	18	Sri Lanka	6
Israel	7	Switzerland	9
Italy	8	Thailand	8
Jamaica	15	Tunisia	20
Kenya	10	Turkey	5

It is difficult to say whether external travel income is more vulnerable than other external income; it probably is. Favorable exchange rates are probably an important factor in attracting tourism.

GOVERNMENT AID

The widespread feeling that foreign aid is shrinking is not confirmed by statistics. The BPS[8] reports that global foreign aid increased by 142 percent from 11.2 billion SDRs in 1974 to 27.1 SDRs in 1980. That is higher than the 128 percent increase in global GER during the same time.

Government aid is, of course, quite uncertain. It can be eliminated with one stroke of the pen. But even this is not as bad as it sounds; recent experience has shown that when a recipient tires of being a client of the West, the East is glad to take over, or vice versa. The analyst should in any case examine closely the extent and the nature of the foreign aid received and assess the consequences of its cancellation. Moreover, the analyst should keep in mind that foreign aid received implies that donations are needed to keep the country going, or that the political situation is precarious, or both.

[8]Ibid.

MANUFACTURED GOODS AS PERCENTAGE OF GER

The IMF published for the first time in the 1982 *IFS Supplement* a series of statistics indicating the percentage of manufactured goods in exports. That adds a useful new tool for creditworthiness analysis.

Previously, analysts had to rely on the *Yearbook of International Trade Statistics*[9] published by the United Nations which indicated separately: Chemicals, Basic Manufactures, Machines, Transportation Equipment, and Miscellaneous Manufactured Goods. The information, however, was practically worthless for credit evaluations because it was published with a time lag of four or five years.

The share represented by exports of manufactured goods in total exports is an important indicator because it shows the degree of economic sophistication of a country. The relevant factor is the higher share of "value added" in manufactured goods.

At present, however, the IFS "Manufactured Goods as Percentage to Exports" data should be looked at with suspicion because for several countries the total percentage of commodity concentrations (listed in a separate table) and manufactured goods exports add up to more than 100. Examples are: Bolivia, Chile, Finland, Jamaica, Malaysia, Sweden, and Zambia listed in the 1982 Supplement. Analysts will have to wait for clarifications that eliminate such inconsistencies before using the new statistical series.

[9]*United Nations Publications*, United Nations, New York, N.Y.

chapter 16

Financial Income and Expenditures (Investment Income)

The "investment income" section of the current account seems to be generally neglected by analysts. That may be due partly to the peculiar phraseology used in the *Balance of Payments Statistics*. The average person, for instance, would not expect to find debit interest on external debt listed among investment income. In an attempt to clarify matters, the wording "financial income and expenditures" is used in this study to indicate "investment income."

Another peculiarity of the *Balance of Payments Statistics* is the use of the word "other."

The investment income section comprises the following items:

11. Reinvested earnings on direct investments abroad.
12. Reinvested earnings on direct investments in the country.
13. Other direct investment income: credit
14. Other direct investment income: debit
15. Other investment income of resident official including interofficial: credit
16. Other investment income of resident official including interofficial: debit
17. Other investment income of foreign official excluding interofficial: credit

18. Other investment income of foreign official excluding interofficial: debit
19. Other investment income: credit
20. Other investment income: debit

That may be summarized in schematic form by separating the reporting country's income items from its expenditure items:

Reporting Country's Income

11.	Earnings on direct investments abroad	–reinvested abroad
13.	Earnings on direct investments abroad	–received from foreign equity holders
15.	Interest earned by official lenders	–from official borrowers
		–from private borrowers
17.	Interest earned by private lenders	–from official borrowers
19.	Interest earned by private lenders	–from private borrowers

Reporting Country's Expenditures

12.	Earnings on direct investments in country	–reinvested in country
14.	Earnings on direct investments in country	–remitted abroad to equity holders
16.	Interest due by official borrowers	–to foreign official lenders
		–to foreign private lenders
18.	Interest due by private borrowers	–to foreign official lenders
20.	Interest due by private borrowers	–to foreign private lenders

DIVIDENDS AND INTEREST

The bulk of investment income is represented by dividends and interest, positive or negative.

Dividends, including stock dividends and bonus shares, represent the distribution of earnings due on the shares and other forms of participation of nonresidents in the equity of incorporated private enterprises, cooperatives, and public corporations. They represent distribution of income.

Interest, including discounts and commitment charges in lieu of interest, comprise income on loans and debt securities, such as bank deposits, bills, bonds, promissory notes, and trade advances. Interest is payable in accordance with a binding agreement between the creditor and the debtor.

Other types of investment income are the earnings of branches and other unincorporated direct investments enterprises, and the direct investor's portion of the earnings of incorporated direct investment enterprises that are not formally distributed.

Earnings from film rentals, charters of mobile equipment, and leases of real estate (rentals) are not classified as investment income. They are included in "Property Income" — items 29 and 30 of the Detailed Presentation.

Some debt securities, such as bonds, notes, and bills, are originally issued at a value different from the stated fixed sum that their holder has the unconditional right to receive when the obligations mature. The premium or discount is regarded as negative interest or additional interest and is shown as investment income.

Direct Investment Income (Items 11 to 14)

The characteristics of direct investments are discussed in chapter 13, BALANCE OF PAYMENTS.

Conceptually, there is the question as to whether both transferred earnings and reinvested earnings should be included in the current account or only transferred earnings.

A. Zuheir Sofia states that " . . . reinvested earnings do not constitute an external service payment burden since they represent foreign capital which is retained in a particular country. . . . It is . . . transferred earnings which could give rise to investment servicing problems of developing countries."[1]

The problem is not as simple as that. The transfer of profits may be postponed for a variety of reasons: exchange restrictions of the country where the business is located, tax reasons or policy considerations of the investor, and so on. Reinvested earnings add to equity holdings of foreigners, and, over time, create new burdens on a country's foreign exchange earnings. The new claims of foreigners have to find a counterpart on the debit side of the current account. That is the method used in the BPS and is the method used for calculations made in this book.

Financial income and expenditures (investment income) not connected with direct investments go under various "other" headings mentioned at the beginning of the chapter.

Official Income (Items 15 to 18)

The *Balance of Payments Manual* states that official income (positive or negative) includes: income receivable or payable by the country's general government or central bank, by a foreign general government or central bank, or by an international organization. State and local governments are included; however, en-

---

[1] A. Zuheir Sofia. *Assessing Country Risk.* Euromoney Publications, London; Chapter 4, Rationalizing Country Risk Ratios, p. 54.

terprises other than the central bank that are operated by the government are excluded.

The reason is that in some countries, Britain, France and Italy for instance, some industries or banks are owned by the government. If the external income of such enterprises were included in "official income," intercountry comparability would suffer.

Official investment income also includes all income payable to, by, or through the IMF. Such income thus covers charges, assessments, interest, and remuneration on transactions and holdings with the IMF, as well as other income receivable by the official sector on reserves.

Other Investment Income (Items 19 and 20)

The credit side of other investment income (item 19) represents mostly interest earned on commercial and business-related loans. It also includes dividends received from portfolio investments abroad, profits of branches abroad, and other investment income received from abroad and not included in previous credit items.

The debit side of other investment income (item 20) represents interest due on money borrowed abroad, portfolio dividends payable abroad, profits of foreign branches in the country, and other financial expenditure abroad not included in previous debit items.

USEFULNESS OF "INVESTMENT INCOME" FOR CREDITWORTHINESS EVALUATION

The financial income and expenditures section of the current account shows the amount contributed to a country's foreign exchange revenues by its international assets (credits and equity holdings abroad and international reserves), and on the other side it indicates the burden caused by foreign liabilities (money borrowed abroad and equity holdings of foreigners).

The size of financial payments received or paid gives an indication of the size of a country's foreign assets or liabilities, and the imbalance between financial income and expenditures indicates in broad terms whether a country's foreign assets exceed its foreign liabilities or vice versa as is more frequently the case.

Other factors being equal, countries that must set aside the highest share of their foreign exchange earnings for interest due to foreign creditors and dividends due to foreign equity holders are more likely to have external payment difficulties, especially if the share of earnings due to foreigners has been increasing over time.

Several ratios relating financial income and expenditures to a country's GER may be calculated. The following will be examined:

A. Total interest due on external debts as percentage of GER.

B. Imbalance between interest due and interest earned on external fixed obligations as percentage of GER.

C. Net investment income (imbalance between interest and dividends due and earned abroad) as percentage of GER.

Another ratio, not related to the GER, is significant as a liquidity indicator:

D. Total interest earned abroad as percentage of total interest due to foreigners.

A—TOTAL INTEREST DUE ON EXTERNAL DEBTS AS PERCENTAGE OF GER

This ratio indicates the share of the GER preempted for payment of interest on external debt. It is no doubt one of the most significant indicators for the creditworthiness analysts.

The trend of the ratio indicates, within broad limits, whether the foreign exchange generating capability of the country is increasing in proportion with the burden created by new obligations, or whether the country's repayment capability is being progressively weakened because the share of the external revenues that has to be set aside for the payment of debit interest is increasing.

It is obvious that if the share of GER preempted by payments of interest due on external obligations continues to increase so that debit interest takes progressively larger shares of foreign exchange earnings, then sooner or later a point will be reached when the burden becomes unbearable.

This is what happened gradually during the past 20 years to some developing countries, as shown in Table 17 listing the two countries out of a sample of 34 countries with the worst "debit interest as percentage of GER" ratios during the two decades 1960 to 1980.

The two worst ratios of the sample are used to indicate the deterioration of the situation because average ratios have little meaning when it becomes a matter of repaying debts; strong debtors are not going to pay the debts of those who cannot pay.

Although no reasonable threshold applicable to all countries may be set for any ratio, it is clear that a ratio cannot keep growing indefinitely. The continuous increase of the interest burden gave plenty of warning of impending difficulties.

Table 17 "Total Interest Due on External Debt as Percentage of GER"—
Two Highest Ratios in a Sample of 34 Countries—Twenty Years 1960–1980.

| | | | | Index Number | |
Year	Second Highest Ratio		Highest Ratio	2nd Highest	Highest
1960	Canada	6.7	Brazil	9.2	100	100
1965	Colombia	7.4	Brazil	9.1	110	99
1970	Mexico	9.4	Colombia	9.8	140	107
1975	Mexico	16.8	Brazil	18.3	251	201
1976	Brazil	18.1	Mexico	18.7	270	203
1977	Brazil	18.0	Mexico	24.6	269	267
1978	Brazil	22.7	Mexico	23.9	339	260
1979	Mexico	23.0	Brazil	28.9	343	314
1980	Bolivia	22.8	Brazil	31.7	340	345

Source: Various issues of *Balance of Payments Yearbook* and *Balance of Payments Statistics.*

As is the case with all indicators, the "total interest due on external debt as percentage of GER" ratio has its weaknesses.

The analyst should be aware that an improvement of the ratio may be caused by renegotiation of the terms of external debts, resulting in lower interest rates. Also the country may have been able to refinance some of the loans obtained from private lenders with soft loans. In any case, the creditors should welcome an improvement of the ratio even if it is not due to a better performance of the country's external accounts.

One problem is that statistics about total debit interest on external obligations are not reported separately in the BPS presentations. Items 16 and 18 represent debit interest. Item 20, on the other hand, includes not only debit interest on external debt, but also interest and dividends payable on portfolio investments of foreigners, earnings of foreign branches in the country, and other investment income due to foreigners not included in items 16 and 18. That, however, should create only minor distortions when developing countries are involved because there equity portfolio investments are practically nonexistent. Dividends on portfolio investments are relevant in only a few countries, such as South Africa where their amount is indicated separately in volume 32 of the *BPS* (2 percent of GER in 1979). Earnings of branches and other residual amounts included in item 20 of the *BPS* should not materially affect the reliability of the ratio.

The total of times 16, 18, and 20 is probably just as good an approximation of external debit interest as any other data available for the computation of other variables (see Chapter 13. under "Net Errors and Omissions").

A Substitute for the Debt Service Ratio

The weaknesses of the commonly used debt service ratio as a performance indicator for creditworthiness evaluation are discussed in Chapter 7, under "The Debt Service Ratio."

John A. Holsen observed in 1977 "As credit from financial institutions, not linked either to particular imports or to progress in project implementation, have become a larger share of debt and debt service, it has become correspondingly easier for borrowers to mobilize new resources which, in effect, offset amortization payments on previous borrowing with comparatively short original maturities. In these circumstances, we are giving increasing attention to the interest burden, and relatively less to the total debt service ratio."[2]

It seems, therefore, appropriate to consider the "Total Interest Due on External Debts as Percentage of GER" ratio as a substitute to replace the debt service ratio (by eliminating amortization from the numerator). The advantages would be:

— the ratio would cease to be a cash flow ratio;
— the numerator would become conceptually sound because income and transfers of funds would not be intermingled;
— the numerator would be conceptually comparable to the denominator because both would exclude transfers of funds;
— inconsistencies due to bunching of maturities would be eliminated.

B—IMBALANCE BETWEEN INTEREST DUE AND INTEREST EARNED ON EXTERNAL FIXED OBLIGATIONS AS PERCENTAGE OF GER

Until the mid-1970s, total debit interest on external borrowing as percentage of GER was probably the most significant indicator for country creditworthiness evaluations.

Subsequently, several countries started to build up their reserves, mostly by borrowing new money abroad. The resulting increases of external debit interest were partly offset by increases of interest earned on international assets.

More than doubling of reserves between the end of 1976 and 1978 in Costa

---

[2]John A. Holsen. "Financing and Risk in Developing Countries." In *Proceedings of a Symposium on Developing Countries' Debt.* Sponsored by the Export Import Bank of the United States, August 1977; Chapter 13, World Bank Techniques for Country Evaluation, p. 103.

Table 18 Imbalance Between External Debit and Credit Interest as Percentage of GER—1978/1980, 1979/1980, and 1980.

Relative Indicator*				1980 Ratio
1978/1980	1979/1980	1980		
Cred. 272	Cred. 269	Cred. 349	Malta	Cred. 11.0
Cred. 333	Cred. 329	Cred. 333	Switzerland	Cred. 10.5
Cred. 82	Cred. 74	Cred. 92	Venezuela	Cred. 2.9
Cred. 55	Cred. 57	Cred. 64	France	Cred. 2.0
Cred. 22	Cred. 31	Cred. 48	United States	Cred. 1.5
Cred. 57	Cred. 49	Cred. 44	Germany	Cred. 1.4
Cred. 20	Cred. 22	Cred. 25	Malaysia	Cred. .8
Cred. 4	Cred. 4	Cred. 10	Syria	Cred. .3
0	0	Cred. 4	Indonesia	Cred. .1
Cred. 20	Cred. 20	0	Japan	0
Cred. 16	Cred. 6	4	Belgium	.1
14	10	6	Cyprus	.2
31	22	19	Italy	.6
65	35	19	Paraguay	.6
16	20	23	Netherlands	.7
25	20	23	Sri Lanka	.7
Cred. 14	Cred. 12	29	Guatemala	.9
14	16	44	United Kingdom	1.4
51	27	44	Kenya	1.4
22	37	48	Tanzania	1.5
65	57	58	Austria	1.8
92	57	60	Egypt	1.9
71	73	89	Greece	2.8
82	88	89	Ireland	2.8
100	78	92	Spain	2.9
106	104	100	Australia	3.2
153	127	100	So. Africa	3.2
127	120	112	Colombia	3.5
100	100	121	Sweden	3.8
153	137	137	Tunisia	4.3
176	165	144	Pakistan	4.5
167	149	150	Finland	4.7
186	178	162	Norway	5.1
163	163	185	Israel	5.8
180	196	198	Thailand	6.2
212	196	204	New Zealand	6.4
186	194	206	Philippines	6.5
192	196	216	Honduras	6.8
212	206	227	Iceland	7.1
231	231	235	Canada	7.4
198	227	287	So. Korea	9.0

(continued)

Table 18 *(Continued)*

Relative Indicator*				1980 Ratio
1978/1980	1979/1980	1980		
272	286	306	Jamaica	9.6
327	331	335	Turkey	10.5
302	321	360	Morocco	11.3
319	341	368	Ecuador	11.6
439	416	422	Chile	13.3
368	416	483	Costa Rica	15.2
368	378	524	Zambia	16.5
586	564	560	Mexico	17.6
551	596	684	Bolivia	21.5
723	768	853	Brazil	26.8

*100 equals median ratio of countries listed; i.e., 3.1 for 1978/1980, 3.2 for 1979/1980, and 3.15 for 1980.
Source: BPS, Vol. 32.

Rica, Ghana, and Paraguay are mentioned in Chapter 6 under, "Accumulation of External Debts and Level of Reserves." Other examples are: Peru, where "Total Reserves minus Gold" quadrupled from the end of 1977 to the end of 1979; Argentina, where they tripled; and Colombia, where they doubled during the same period (*IFS*, December 1981).

By the end of the Seventies, "Imbalance Between Interest Due and Interest Earned on External Fixed Obligations as Percentage of GER" became a more representative performance ratio for creditworthiness evaluations.

Table 18 reports "Imbalance Between Interest Due and Interest Earned on External Fixed Obligations as Percentage of GER" for 51 countries for the years 1978 to 1980.

The first three columns report relative indicators in which 100 equals the median of the countries listed for the periods 1978/80, 1979/80, and 1980. The fourth column reports 1980 ratios. The countries are listed on the basis of increasing 1980 ratios.

C—NET INVESTMENT INCOME (IMBALANCE BETWEEN INTEREST PLUS IMBALANCE BETWEEN DIVIDENDS DUE AND EARNED ABROAD) AS PERCENTAGE OF GER

Ratio B, "Imbalance Between Interest Due and Interest Earned on External Fixed Obligations as Percentage of GER", does not reflect the burden imposed on or the contribution made to GER by profits on foreign investments. Equity investment earnings, whether due or receivable, have to be included in the computation in order to obtain an overall picture of the effects of foreign assets and liabilities on the external earnings and expenditures of a country.

Some analysts may be inclined to overlook the burden imposed on external revenues by earnings on direct investment of foreigners. But as the following short list shows, including, or excluding, earnings due on foreign direct investments may change a country's picture considerably.

	Interest (1)	Interest Plus Equity Earnings (2)	(2) As Percentage of (1) (3)
Greece	2.8	2.8	100
Ireland	2.8	2.8	100
Honduras	6.8	14.5	213
Australia	3.2	10.5	328

(1) Imbalance of interest on external fixed obligations as percentage of GER.
(2) External interest imbalance plus equity earnings imbalance as percentage of GER.
(3) Interest plus equity earnings as percentage of interest.

It is clear that earnings on equity investments abroad, and earnings of foreigners having equity investments in the country, should both be included in the computation if an overall picture is wanted.

Table 19   Net Investment Income—Imbalance Between Interest and Dividends Due and Earned Abroad—as Percentage of GER—1978/1980, 1979/1980 and 1980.

Relative Indicator*						
1978/1980		1979/1980		1980		1980 Ratio
Cred.	186	Cred.	188	Cred.	171	Switzerland	Cred.	10.5
Cred.	183	Cred.	186	Cred.	154	United States	Cred.	9.5
Cred.	108	Cred.	110	Cred.	142	Malta	Cred.	8.8
Cred.	30	Cred.	39	Cred.	35	France	Cred.	2.2
Cred.	11	Cred.	12	Cred.	24	Venezuela	Cred.	1.5
Cred.	18	Cred.	18	Cred.	8	Japan	Cred.	.5
Cred.	18	Cred.	15	Cred.	8	Germany	Cred.	.5
Cred.	2	Cred.	1	Cred.	4	Syria	Cred.	.3
Cred.	17	Cred.	12		0	United Kingdom		0
Cred.	9	Cred.	3		1	Belgium		.1
	3		3		4	Netherlands		.3
	18		12		10	Italy		.6
	21		16		13	Cyprus		.8

(continued)

Table 19 *(Continued)*

Relative Indicator*				1980 Ratio
1978/1980	1979/1980	1980		
20	21	24	Tanzania	1.5
23	22	24	Sri Lanka	1.5
47	27	28	Egypt	1.7
36	31	30	Austria	1.8
39	40	45	Greece	2.8
47	49	45	Ireland	2.8
36	34	51	Guatemala	3.1
64	48	51	Spain	3.1
52	54	62	Sweden	3.8
100	85	73	Colombia	4.5
100	97	75	Pakistan	4.6
98	92	83	Finland	5.1
98	100	100	Israel	6.2
106	116	107	Thailand	6.6
138	133	107	Norway	6.6
133	130	110	New Zealand	6.8
161	133	117	Kenya	7.2
138	130	118	So. Africa	7.3
167	150	133	Tunisia	8.2
152	115	135	Paraguay	8.3
162	159	141	Canada	8.7
147	148	142	Philippines	8.8
115	133	148	So. Korea	9.1
147	158	149	Iceland	9.2
158	159	154	Malaysia	9.5
194	189	171	Australia	10.5
186	195	179	Turkey	11.0
171	206	200	Morocco	12.3
283	264	231	Indonesia	14.3
239	247	235	Honduras	14.5
267	253	237	Chile	14.6
277	280	265	Ecuador	16.3
229	215	268	Zambia	16.5
274	279	269	Jamaica	16.6
239	261	271	Costa Rica	16.7
427	416	368	Mexico	22.9
353	381	378	Bolivia	23.3
532	530	485	Brazil	29.9

*100 equals median ratio of countries listed; i.e., 5.6 for 1978/1980, 5.6 for 1979/1980, and 6.2 for 1980.
Source: *BPS*, Vol. 32.

The ratio relates the burden caused by past current account deficits to the foreign exchange generating capability of a country. In that sense it shows how successful a government's policies are in managing current account deficits and keeping them within the limits of a country's foreign exchange earning capabilities.

Table 19 reports "Net Investment Income (imbalance between interest and dividends due and earned abroad) as percentage of GER" for 51 countries for the years 1978 to 1980.

The first three columns report relative indicators in which 100 equals the median of the countries listed for the periods 1978/80, 1979/80, and 1980. The fourth column reports 1980 ratios. The countries are listed on the basis of increasing 1980 ratios.

Table 20   Total Interest Earned Abroad as Percentage of Total Interest Due to Foreigners—1980.

	Percent	Relative Indicator*		Percent	Relative Indicator*
Malta	1,571.4	3,680	Sweden	41.9	98
Germany	139.7	327	Norway	39.0	91
Malaysia	132.7	311	Philippines	36.3	85
Indonesia	123.0	288	Tunisia	35.6	83
France	120.8	283	Finland	33.8	79
United States	115.5	270	Thailand	32.3	76
Japan	100.3	235	Honduras	27.8	65
Paraguay	95.2	223	Canada	26.5	62
Cyprus	92.9	218	Chile	26.1	61
Netherlands	92.0	215	Pakistan	24.4	57
United Kingdom	83.8	196	So. Africa	22.3	52
Austria	82.6	193	So. Korea	20.1	47
Guatemala	81.7	191	Ecuador	19.6	46
Egypt	71.4	167	Mexico	18.3	43
Colombia	70.2	164	Brazil	15.4	36
Ireland	68.7	161	Iceland	13.0	30
Morocco	68.6	161	Australia	12.1	28
Sri Lanka	64.3	151	New Zealand	10.3	24
Spain	58.7	138	Jamaica	7.1	17
Kenya	58.2	136	Costa Rica	7.0	16
Israel	58.2	136	Bolivia	5.6	13
Tanzania	52.4	123	Zambia	1.7	4
Greece	42.7	100			

*100 equals median of countries listed, i.e. 42.7.
Source: *BPS*, Vol. 32.

D—TOTAL INTEREST EARNED ABROAD AS PERCENTAGE OF TOTAL INTEREST DUE TO FOREIGNERS

The ratio indicates whether, in addition to reserves, a country or its residents have funds abroad that could be used in case of emergency (see Chapter 4, under "Liquidity Problems").

The relationship between interest earned abroad and interest due on external obligations broadly reflects a country's international financial situation.

A low "interest earned to interest due" ratio indicates that a country does not have much to fall back on in case of need. From that viewpoint, and keeping in mind that it may not be possible to collect some of the money lent to developing countries in time, the ratio may be used as a secondary liquidity indicator.

Table 20 reports "Total Interest Earned Abroad as Percentage of Total Interest Due to Foreigners" for 45 countries for the year 1980. The relative indicator is based on the median of the countries listed (median equals 100).

chapter 17

Per Capita Income and Population Increases

The assessment of political risk should come last in a country's creditworthiness evaluation.

One should first examine a country's past international economic performance and ascertain its external repayment capability. That is discussed in chapters 11 to 16. The practical reliability of some of the procedures that were taken into consideration is tested in Chapter 19, EXPERIMENTAL TESTING—CONCLUSIONS.

A relatively poor past performance in the international held means that the lender is facing a relatively poor international credit risk. One may hope that favorable political or economic developments may improve the situation, but that may be only wishful thinking.

If, on the other hand, past international economic performance is good, the big question is: Will that continue? That depends essentially on a country's political and economic structure and on exogenous developments.

The problems caused in the past by exogenous factors are reflected in the "GER Instability Index;" the potential vulnerability of foreign exchange earnings to exogenous factors is reflected in the "GER Concentration Index" (both are discussed in Chapter 15).

Past experience is, of course, only an indication of what may happen. The range of future commodity swings (including petroleum and gold) is unpredictable. One may, however, reasonably assume that countries that had more stable earnings in the past will probably be less affected in the future by unfavorable exogenous factors.

POLITICAL STABILITY

The assessment of political stability is essentially a subjective process. Most human actions are unpredictable, therefore, most political events are also unpredictable.

Two approaches are commonly used to evaluate political stability.

One consists of checklists of a number of variables, such as government change procedures, regime stability, power of political opposition groups, ethnic conflicts, and so on. An overall score of political risk is then calculated by assigning weights to each variable, and by scoring each variable (see Chapter 8, under "Political Risk Forecasts").

The systematic analysis of political factors is helpful because it brings together information and opinions generated by various sources. The problem with this approach is that, notwithstanding its scientific appearance, the end result of the procedure is still a summary of subjective judgments.

PER CAPITA INCOME

The other approach to the problem of evaluation political stability takes into consideration per capita income levels.

The underlying concept is that high per capita incomes are the cumulative result of many factors which favor economic growth. Among them: good economic institutions, formation of sufficient capital for economic expansion, availability of technically trained personnel (engineers, administrators, educators, reasonably efficient public officials, and so on) who will be there to help solve problems and difficulties which will inevitably arise. Countries with high per capita incomes have surmounted the difficult stage of initial economic development when capital formation is insufficient and the population tends to become impatient with existing institutions.

Economic development, on the other hand, does not take place in a vacuum; it is part of an evolutionary process which brings with it also more sophisticated and more stable social and political institutions. In industrial countries, basic political changes are usually gradual. On the other hand, some developing countries have one-man governments, or governments in the hands of a few individuals. Since no one knows what will happen when the leader dies, or is compelled to leave the country in a hurry, it should be obvious that such countries present a higher degree of political risk.

The level of per capita income may offer an indirect answer to the bothersome question of the future political stability of a country. Higher per capita income levels would normally indicate a smaller probability of sudden political change that may adversely affect external creditors.

Incidentally, whether the GDP or the GNP is used to calculate per capita income is unimportant; the differences between the two calculations are too small to warrant attention. The GDP is used in this chapter for per capita income computations since, in some instances, it is reported before GNP.

However, several problems have to be solved before a valid comparison of per capita incomes can be made.

The first one concerns the rate of exchange to be used. National incomes are reported in local currency. In order to make comparisons, per capita incomes must be converted into a currency used as common denominator, usually the dollar. With floating rates of exchange and periodic devaluations, it is difficult to obtain consistent comparisons.

One good example is given by the 1976 Mexican devaluation. For the year 1975, Mexico's per capita income was 9,174 pesos, which at 12.50 pesos per dollar was the equivalent of 734 dollars; however, at the end of 1976, after the devaluation, the rate was 19.95 pesos to the dollar, reducing the equivalent to 460 dollars. Which figure represents the amount which should be compared with the per capita income of other countries? Probably neither one; the answer is probably somewhere between the two figures.

The drastic 1976 Mexican peso devaluation is not an exception. In some instances foreign exchange rates remain unchanged for a considerable period of time while the purchasing power of the domestic currency is gradually eroded. To compensate, at least partially, for this lack of synchronization between the loss of domestic purchasing power of a currency and its exchange rate adjustments, one may use, for instance, three-year average per capita incomes, converted into dollars at the average rate of exchange of the three-year period.

PURCHASING POWER PARITY

An even bigger problem is to determine the real domestic purchasing power of the local currency and to establish what is technically known as purchasing power parity.

The World Bank Annual Report 1981, for instance, mentions that International Development Association assistance is ". . . concentrated on the very poor countries—mainly those with annual per capita gross national product of less than $681 (in 1979 dollars). More than 70 countries are eligible under this criterion."[1]. Since income distribution is uneven in all countries, one may safely assume that a good part of the population has to survive on half the average amount.

In the United States, on the other hand, the government definition of poverty (1983) is a family of four living on less than $9,862 a year; adjusted to 1979 prices that is about $7,300, or $1,825 per person. It is clear that anyone trying to live in the United States on $300 or $400 a year would either die of starvation or freeze to death, whichever comes first.

[1]World Bank Annual Report 1981, p. 3.

Most people with very low per capita income live in warm climates where no heating is needed. But that is only part of the explanation. The answer is that there are wide disparities between "nominal per capita income" (obtained by converting the local currency into dollars at the prevailing exchange rates) and "real per capita income" (based on domestic purchasing power of the local currency).

Theoretically, freely floating exchange rates should, over a period of time, tend to equalize the domestic price levels of internationally traded goods and services. However most goods consumed internally in developing countries are not traded internationally. As a result, nominal incomes may be completely different from per capita incomes in real terms.

The problem is to find a comparative index that reflects the real cost of living in each country in terms of local currency. The index should be based on a detailed survey of prices in each country so that purchasing power parity could be calculated. Of course, it is not feasible to include all goods and services in the comparison; therefore, a selection of what should be included in each basket—one for each country—will have to be made on a subjective basis. Moreover, a weight will have to be assigned to each component.

Apart from the subjective nature of the basket's formula, the real problem is that such studies are very time consuming, and, as a result, are usually very much out of date when ready.

A 1978 United Nations study, for instance, reported (eight years late) 1970 average price levels in India—calculated on the basis of prevailing rates of exchange—as being only 30 percent of the United States level.[2]

That is not unique. More recently, on May 19, 1983, *The Wall Street Journal* reported that the World Bank's *Atlas* lists Hungary's income at $4,180 per person. However, World Bank officials are following an IMF decision to accept Hungary's own income estimate of $2,100 per capita (which would qualify the country for a World Bank loan). A United States Treasury study concludes that Hungary's income per capita was between $3,809 and $6,399 in 1981 "and most probably that it was nearer the upper end of this range than the lower . . ." (as quoted by *The Wall Street Journal*).

In brief, estimates of Hungary's per capita income were:

	Amount	Index*
National estimate	$2,100	100
As listed in World Bank Atlas	$4,180	199
U.S. Treasury study:		
Low	$3,809	181
High	$6,399	305
*National estimate equals 100.		

[2]*Economic Journal of the United Nations*, June 1978. "Real GDP Per Capita for More than One Hundred Countries," by Irving Kravis, Alan Weston, and Robert Summers; as reported by The Economist, London, July 22, 1978, p. 70.

The reader will notice the bureaucratic exactitude of the Treasury: from $3,809 to $6,399 and not from $3,800 to $6,400 as anyone with common sense would have said.

PETROLEUM EXPORTING COUNTRIES

Another problem, if one wants to use per capita income as an indicator of economic maturity, is that in some countries petroleum exports, or exports of minerals, make up a good share of GNP.

That the United Arab Emirates had a per capita income of more than $40,000 in 1980, or that Kuwait had one of more than $20,000, reflects the accidental ownership of large petroleum fields combined with a relatively small population, rather than economic maturity leading to political stability. The fact that petroleum exporting countries have a high external repayment potential does not mean that they are necessarily politically stable, as shown, for instance, by what happened in Iran.

The analyst may try to recompute per capita incomes of petroleum exporting countries by deducting petroleum exports from the computation, in which case the United Arab Emirates' per capita income would come down to $13,900, while Kuwait's would go down to $9,800. Even such per capita incomes would place the countries well above their respective economic development stage.

To conclude, it is obvious that, due to the guessing generally involved in GDP calculations and the guesses involved in converting domestic purchasing power in other currencies, per capita income in its present form should be used with circumspection as a creditworthiness evaluation tool.

PER CAPITA INCOME TREND OVER TIME

Although a comparison of per capita income levels may be misleading, a comparison of per capita income trends over time should be more reliable because identical procedures will probably be used in each country to calculate successive income data.

For creditworthiness evaluation purposes, recent trends of per capita incomes are probably more significant than their absolute level.

The trend of per capita income indicates whether the combined effects of a country's structure and of its savings policies are able to overcome the problems created by high birth rates.

One should, therefore, examine recent per capita income trends and, subsequently, look at birth rates, which are the most intractable problem in most underdeveloped countries.

Table 21 reports "Average yearly per capita income increases (or decreases)

Table 21 Average Yearly Per Capita Income Increase in Real Terms—
1978/ 1980.

	Rate	Relative Indicator*		Rate	Relative Indicator*
Malta	9.26	383	Belgium	2.29	95
Paraguay	8.22	340	So. Africa	2.24	93
Cyrpus	6.94	287	Switzerland	2.18	90
Chile	6.57	271	Ireland	2.11	87
Egypt	6.45	267	Sweden	2.09	86
Mexico	6.40	264	Ecuador	1.92	79
Thailand	5.89	243	Honduras	1.58	65
Malysia	5.84	241	Australia	1.51	62
Finland	5.08	210	Costa Rica	1.44	60
Indonesia	5.08	210	Canada	1.32	55
Tunisia	4.85	200	Guatemala	1.30	54
Sri Lanka	4.34	179	Israel	1.29	53
Japan	4.26	176	Netherlands	1.10	45
Norway	3.94	163	United Kingdom	1.07	44
Syria	3.89	161	New Zealand	.97	40
Brazil	3.74	155	United States	.95	39
Italy	3.59	148	Morocco	.66	27
Colombia	3.44	142	Kenya	.52	21
Pakistan	3.44	142	Spain	.20	8
So. Korea	3.28	136	Tanzania	.20	8
Germany	3.27	135	Bolivia	−.76	−31
Philippines	3.20	132	Turkey	−1.82	−75
Iceland	2.99	124	Venezuela	−2.07	−86
Austria	2.95	122	Jamaica	−3.61	−149
Greece	2.90	120	Zambia	−4.27	−176
France	2.42	100			

*100 equals median ratio of countries listed; i.e., 2.42 per cent per annum.
Source: *IFS*, December 1981.

in real terms for the years 1978 to 1980." The first column lists the rate and the second column lists the relative indicator (100 equals median of countries listed).

It is questionable whether some of the higher per capita income increases shown by developing countries should be taken at face value.

The decline of per capita income in Zambia, Jamaica, Turkey and Bolivia, looks ominous especially since they came with deficits in the current account.

POPULATION INCREASES

An increasing population creates the immediate problem of more mouths to feed and the inevitable problem of finding jobs years later when the young people become of working age.

Developing countries usually go through a transition period when infant mortality drops sharply due to better sanitation, but birth rates remain high with the result of an accelerated increase of population. The transition period ends when overall death rates stop falling and birth rates begin to decline. That usually

Table 22   Average Yearly Population Increases (%)—1978–1980.

	Rate	Relative Indicator*		Rate	Relative Indicator*
New Zealand	−.11	−6	Tanzania	1.99	104
Austria	−.04	−2	Malta	2.10	110
United Kingdom	.02	1	Malaysia	2.31	121
Germany	.09	5	Indonesia	2.38	125
Belgium	.10	5	Israel	2.40	126
Switzerland	.21	11	Tunisia	2.42	127
Sweden	.24	13	Turkey	2.60	137
Finland	.28	15	Costa Rica	2.74	143
Italy	.34	18	Egypt	2.75	144
France	.40	21	Bolivia	2.84	149
Norway	.41	21	So. Africa	2.91	152
Iceland	.45	24	Philippines	2.99	157
Netherlands	.70	37	Venezuela	3.06	160
Cyprus	.82	43	Guatemala	3.17	166
Japan	.85	45	Brazil	3.20	168
Canada	.94	49	Paraguay	3.21	168
Spain	.99	52	Colombia	3.29	172
Greece	1.19	62	Zambia	3.33	174
Australia	1.30	68	Pakistan	3.37	176
Ireland	1.33	70	Morocco	3.41	179
Jamaica	1.43	75	Ecuador	3.48	182
So. Korea	1.61	84	Honduras	3.71	194
United States	1.65	86	Mexico	3.78	198
Chile	1.74	91	Syria	3.99	209
Thailand	1.83	96	Kenya	4.79	250
Sri Lanka	1.91	100			

*100 equals median population increase of countries listed, i.e., 1.91 percent per annum.
Source: *IFS*, December 1981.

happens when the country reaches a higher level of economic development (which, incidentally, has not been defined since it varies from country to country).

If the economy does not grow faster than the expanding population, per capita income remains stagnant or declines in real terms. At that stage, people tend to become impatient; they are more willing to support political unrest, and their government is more willing to engage in economic experimentation which may adversely affect foreign creditors.

As mentioned above, the adverse effects of high birth rates will be felt for years to come (probably 15 to 20) until productive jobs are found for the new entrants in the labor force.

Table 22 reports "Average yearly population increases for the years 1978-1980." The first column lists the rate of increase; the second lists the relative indicator (100 equals median of countries listed).

chapter 18

Warning Signals

Most analysts would be interested in finding a system intended to flash some kind of warning signal of impending drastic changes in a country's political situation.

The news media, of course, prominently feature any adverse event, whether domestic or international. From that source the analyst receives plenty of warnings. The problem, however, is that practically no international loans would be granted if all unfavorable news media reports were taken at their face value. The banks would have to get out of the international lending business.

The search, therefore, should be for some phenomenon which is generally associated with drastic political changes. One logical candidate for the signaling job would be capital flight. One would assume that when conditions get really bad, the well informed would accelerate the transfer of their money to a safe haven. If one could spot the acceleration of capital flight abroad, one may obtain a significant signal.

The items to watch would be "Net Errors and Omissions" (N.E.&O.) and "Reserves." Another symptom would be any unusual delay with which statistical data are reported.

As explained in Chapter 13 THE BALANCE OF PAYMENTS, the principles used in compiling balance of payments result in a body of positive and negative entries whose totals should balance. In practice, however, there will inevitably be an imbalance between the two totals. In theory, the residual item N.E.&O. is the result of errors and inconsistencies in the estimates and of omissions from the statement; actually it may also represent illegal transfers of money that cannot be traced, and therefore show up in the balance of payments computation as N.E.&O.

A good example is Switzerland which is the only industrial country showing N.E.&O. (on the credit side) in excess of ten percent of its gross external revenues, plus 14 percent in 1977, plus 25 percent in 1978, and plus 21 percent in 1979.[1]

Evidently, a good share of the unofficial money transfers into Switzerland—presumably transferred illegally from the country of origin—cannot be traced even by the very efficient Swiss.

The problem with the N.E.&O. item, as a warning signal, is that there is a considerable time lag before the balance of payments statistics are published, so that its effectiveness as a warning signal is lost.

On the other hand, if the flight of capital is heavy enough, and if the ruling group sees the writing on the wall, the flight may be reflected in an unusual drop of reserves not associated with balance of payments difficulties.

Did the level of reserves flash any such warning signals before some of the recent drastic government changes took place that affected the country's creditworthiness? Examples that come to mind are Cuba, Ethiopia, Afghanistan, Iran, and Nicaragua.

CUBA

Cuba is an interesting case. Castro took over at the beginning of 1959, and at first some observers considered him an "agrarian reformer" rather than a Marxist revolutionary.

In the middle of 1957, Cuba's official reserves were high enough to pay for seven months of foreign expenditures (including merchandise imports, services, and other invisibles). During the preceding three years, the average 12-month variations (comparison of each month's total with the total of the same month of the previous year) of the reserves was 4 percent, indicating that the reserves were quite steady. At the end of September 1957, reserves were 6 percent above the average of the previous three years. It seemed that things were in good order.

However, the following table, prepared with IFS statistics, shows some suspicious changes, starting with October 1957:

Cuba—Official Reserves

	Month-to-Month Variations		12 Month Variations	
1957—May	up	4.0%	down	3.0%
June	up	2.5%	up	.2%
July		0	up	.2%

Cuba—Official Reserves (*Continued*)

	Month-to-Month Variations		12 Month Variations	
1957—Aug.	down	.9%	down	.2%
Sept.	down	4.5%	down	2.7%
Oct.	down	7.1%	down	8.2%
Nov.	down	1.7%	down	5.7%
Dec.	down	4.5%	down	7.9%
1958—Jan.	down	.4%	down	6.2%
Feb.	down	.2%	down	7.6%
Mar.	down	.5%	down	8.6%
Apr.	down	1.4%	down	14.3%
May	up	.7%	down	17.0%
June	down	2.1%	down	20.1%
July	down	.9%	down	21.5%

(up to and including November, 1958, IFS)

The month-to-month changes are inclusive. The picture was obscured by seasonal increases of foreign exchange receipts (sugar, representing almost 80 percent of the exports, and tourism).

The 12-month changes, however indicated in October 1957—when reserves dropped more than twice the four percent average fluctuations of the previous three years—that some unfavorable developments were taking place. By March 1958 (nine months before Castro took over), the unusual deterioration of reserve levels was confirmed by six consecutive above-average declines. The September 1958 IFS reported further drops of 14 and 17 percent for April and May, indicating that the flight of capital was getting worse.

ETHIOPIA

The case of Ethiopia is more complicated. The military seized power on June 29, 1974, Hailie Selassie was deposed on September 12, 1974, and the Marxist junta seized power on November 24, 1974. Which event precipitated the radical political changes which took place after the Emperor was deposed? Which event should have been taken as a warning signal?

The prudent lender should have considered the taking over of power by the military on June 29, 1974, after a very long absolute reign of the Emperor, as a strong warning signal of impending drastic political changes. The analysis of the reserve statistics, however, does not show any warning signals. Moreover, statistical reporting to the IMF was up to date.

AFGHANISTAN

In Afghanistan, there was a military coup during April, 1978, which brought a Marxist pro-Soviet party to power. The coup was followed by various changes in the composition of the pro-Soviet government which led to the Russian intervention of January, 1980. There were no suspicious changes in reserves, as a matter of fact, in April, 1978, reserves were almost at twice the level of the previous year. There was no unusual increase in the time lag with which the statistics were reported to the IMF. The seizing of power by a pro-Soviet government should have been taken as a warning signal.

IRAN

After a considerable period of political unrest, the Shah left Iran in January, 1979. There was a decline of reserves starting in March, 1978, after they reached the unprecedented level of thirteen and one half billion dollars (up from the eight billion level in March 1976). Statistics were reported promptly. IFS statistics gave no warning signal.

NICARAGUA

In Nicaragua, however, there were two statistical warning signals. Somoza left the country in July, 1979. By using the same technique applied to the analysis of Cuba's reserves, namely by comparing the monthly reserve figures with those of the same month of the preceding year, one detects 15 months before Somoza's departure a first warning signal in January, 1978 (March 1978 IFS), strongly confirmed in the subsequent months. The month-to-month comparison of the reserve figures is obviously inconclusive. Another warning signal was that the reporting of reserve statistics was falling behind.

Nicaragua—Official Reserves

	Month-to-month variations		12 month variations	
1978—Jan.	down	3.4%	down	6.9%
Feb.	down	1.5%	down	23.1%
Mar.	up	7.6%	down	29.7%
Apr.	up	.4%	down	31.4%
May	down	4.5%	down	26.5%
June	down	6.6%	down	41.2%
July	down	13.0%	down	37.8%
Aug.	down	4.0%	down	47.5%
Sept.	down	8.3%	down	55.3%
Oct.	down	7.4%	down	59.4%

Nicaragua—Official Reserves (*Continued*)

	Month-to-month variations		12 month variations	
1978—Nov.	down	4.1%	down	53.3%
Dec.	up	13.7%	down	65.2%
1979—Jan.		delayed		
Feb.		delayed		
Mar.		delayed		
Apr.		delayed		

(up to and including June, 1979, IFS)

It seems that it would be worthwhile to compare regularly 12-month reserve variations with the average variations of the previous three years. The one-year warning for Cuba and a 15-month warning for Nicaragua, given by reserve statistics, would have been useful.

There is a further lesson: month-to-month variations will tend to camouflage even a disastrous trend like the one in Nicaragua's reserves.

chapter 19

Experimental Testing—Conclusions

Testing past country evaluations against subsequent performance is not as easy as it may seem.

Looking at the pre-World War II period one finds, for instance, that about 800 bond issues from 43 countries were placed in the United States during the 1920s, for a value of over $7 billion. During that period no bonds defaulted except two Brazilian state issues.[1] A few years later almost all bonds went into default during the great depression. Bonds which were considered safe became almost worthless and creditworthiness evaluation procedures which appeared to be excellent proved to be wrong.

In the post-World War II period there were only a few Cuba style defaults or outright refusals to pay external obligations following a communist takeover of a country's government, so few of them that, up to a few years ago, most observers considered default a very remote possibility. On the other hand there have been numerous reschedulings, but creditors did not suffer any material losses.

How is one to judge past risk evaluations? Against defaults which up to now did not materialize, or against reschedulings which did not cause losses?

It would seem that the problem of testing the validity of past evaluations should be approached from a different viewpoint. Instead of relating past eval-

---

[1]Ilse Mintz. *Deterioration in the Quality of Foreign Bonds Issued in the United States 1920-1930*, National Bureau of Economic Research, Inc., New York, N.Y., pp 10 and 29.

uations to rare default or more frequent reschedulings, one should compare them with assessments made subsequently, after some unexpected event such as the August 1982 Mexican payment difficulties which prompted lenders to take a closer look at their portfolios. This will be attempted in the following pages.

Data published in the 1981 *Yearbook* of the *Balance of Payments Statistics* and in 1981 issues of the *International Financial Statistics* (IFS) are used to make a set of experimental country external repayment risk evaluations, based on comparable data.

The external repayment risk evaluations are then compared with the March 1982 Institutional Investor Country Credit Ratings, which reflect the prevalent judgments of international commercial banks at the same time. The experimental evaluations are also compared with March 1983 and September 1983 Institutional Investor ratings to determine whether they have any predictive qualities.

The 1981 experimental evaluations would have given approximately a six-month warning before the Mexican payment difficulties. To determine whether a longer warning could have been given, a new set of experimental evaluations was made on the basis of 1980 BPS and IFS data and then compared with March 1982, March 1983, and September 1983 Institutional Investor ratings.

SCOPE OF EXPERIMENTAL TESTING

Experimental evaluations are limited to the "Comparable Factual Data" section of the suggested country report (see Chapter 11, under "Suggested Outline of Report"). The "Judgmental Economic Factors" and "Judgmental Social and Political Factors" sections and "Conclusions" are excluded from the test, since they are not based on comparable factual data.

Since the post-1982 international payment difficulties are not caused by social or political factors but by economic factors, countries which had relatively poor foreign exchange generating capability, and/or were heavily overspending, and/or were burdened by relatively heavy external obligations, were those that were going to have external payment difficulties when global conditions deteriorated. Their external accounts should have shown signs of weaknesses which should be reflected in their external repayment risk indicators.

The experimental evaluations are based on data reported in the following tables:

Table 12—Gross External Revenues (GER) Percentage Increase 1978/1980–1979/1980–1980.

Table 13—Gross External Revenues (GER) Instability Index–1971–1980.

Table 16—Sum of Squares GER Concentration Index - 1978/1980–1979/1980–1980.

Table 9—Current Account Imbalance as Percentage of Gross External Revenues (GER)–Averages 1978/1980 - Averages 1979/1980–1980.

Table 10—Current Account Imbalance as Percentage of Gross External Revenues (GER) Increases–Averages 1978/1980–1979/1980–1980.

Table 18—Imbalance Between External Debit and Credit Interest as Percentage of GER–1978/1980–1979/1980–1980.

Table 19—Net Investment Income—Imbalance Between Interest and Dividends Due and Earned Abroad—as Percentage of GER–1978/1980–1979/1980–1980.

Table 20—Total Interest Earned Abroad as Percentage of Total Interest Due to Foreigners—1980.

Table 3—Credit Balances as Percentage of Amounts Due to Banks Reporting to the Bank for International Settlements (BIS)—September 30, 1981.

Table 21—Average Yearly Per Capita Income Increase in Real Terms—1978/1980.

Table 22—Average Yearly Population Increase (%)—1978/1980.

Table 7—Dollar Adjusted CPI Increase as Percentage of Dollar Rate of Exchange Increase—1978/1980 (Relative Purchasing Power Indicator).

The procedures outline in the previous chapters 11 to 17 are followed to calculate the following indicators:

Factual Repayment Risk Indicator
  1. Relative GER generating capability
      –GER increascs
      –GER instability indicator
      –GER concentration indicator
  2. Overspending habits
      –Current account imbalance percent GER
      –Current account imbalance percent GER increase
  3. External financial burden
      –Imbalance external interest percent GER
      –Imbalance external interest plus imbalance equity earnings percent GER

Liquidity Risk Indicator
  1. External interest earned percent interest due
  2. Credit balances with banks percent of amount due to banks reporting to BIS

Per Capita Income Increase—Population Increase Risk Indicator
  1. Per capita income increase
  2. Population increase

Purchasing Power Change Risk Indicator

(Dollar adjusted CPI change percent of dollar exchange rate adjustment.)

Only the External Repayment Risk Indicator has been used for comparisons with Institutional Investor Ratings because no reasonable system has been found to incorporate it into a comprehensive indicator with the other indicators.

Liquidity Risk Indicators, Per Capita Income Increase and Population Increase Risk Indicators, and Purchasing Power Change Risk Indicators are used in "Comparable Factual Country Risk Profiles" of which four examples are given after Repayment Risk/Institutional Investor comparisons.

TECHNICAL PROBLEMS

Some of the indicators used in credit evaluations have positive value, for example increase of external revenues or increase of per capita incomes, while other indicators have negative value, for example GER instability indicator or the ratio of current account deficit as percentage of GER.

Since the majority of the indicators used in the experimental testing have negative value, the reciprocals of positive indicators are used in the calculations in order to have easily comparable figures. That means, for instance, that an increase of external revenues representing 50 percent of the median increase in a group of countries is included in the computations as a 200 risk indicator (200 being the reciprocal of 50).

As a result of this procedure the indicators reported in the following pages are risk indicators, not creditworthiness indicators.

To facilitate comparisons, all indicators used in the following presentation equal 100 of the median of the countries included in the sample. The reader can see immediately, without consulting other references, whether any variable of any country is below or above par.

One of the most baffling decisions is the selection of the base period to be used for the evaluation. Trends and ratios change continuously and the analyst does not know which one may prevail in the future (see Chapter 11, under "Selection of Base Period").

It is obviously arbitrary to select one period as being representative of the underlying situation. Somewhat less arbitrary is a system in which several base periods are used. The highest and the lowest ratios or indicators of the periods selected are then used to define an evaluation range, the assumption being that a correct evaluation will probably fall within the range indicated. The spread between high and low of the evaluation range is an indicator of the uncertainty of the evaluation (see Chapter 11, under "Multiple Evaluations").

The three-year period 1978/80, for which data were available at the end of 1981, is selected as a basis for the experimental "External Repayment Risk" indicators, for which multiple evaluations, based on the periods 1978/80, 1979/80, and 1980, are calculated. For the "GER Instability" indicator for which a ten-year base period is recommended, 1971/80 is used. Only one evaluation, based on most recent data available, is made for "Liquidity" indicators, for "Per Capita Income Increase," and "Population Increase Risk" indicators and for the "Purchasing Power Change Risk" indicator.

WEIGHTS

The most controversial decision involved in the evaluation process is the selection of weights to be attributed to each component in order to arrive at a composite risk indicator. There is no logical way of determining, for instance, the inter-relationship of the components of the External Repayment Risk indicator. The seven variables used for the calculation of the indicator will inevitably give inconsistent, sometimes conflicting, signals.

Which one of the three kinds of variables, GER Generating Capability, Overspending Habits, and External Financial Burden, is more important? These are very difficult questions. Poor foreign exchange generating capability means poor repayment capacity; on the other hand, overspending can fritter away any amount of GER; finally, the burden caused by external obligations may be so heavy that it may become unbearable.

A closer look at the seven components of the repayment risk indicator shows that three of the variables, GER Increase, Current Account Imbalance as Percentage of GER, and Current Account Imbalance as Percentage of GER Increase, reflect temporary phenomena because foreign exchange revenues do not increase at a steady rate over time, and a current account deficit in one year may be followed by a surplus the next year.

On the other hand the other four variables, the ten-year Instability Indicator, the GER Concentration Indicator, the Imbalance External Interest as Percentage of GER, and the Imbalance External Interest plus Imbalance Equity Earnings as Percentage of GER, reflect more basic conditions. The degree of concentration of foreign exchange earnings changes slowly over time, interest on external debt does not increase or decrease suddenly, and that applies also, although to a lesser degree, to foreign equity earnings.

To reflect the basic difference between the two kinds of variables, the three "temporary phenomena" indicators are included in the experimental repayment risk indicator calculation for one half of their value, while the four indicators reflecting "more basic conditions" are included in the computation for their full value.

That, of course, is an arbitrary decision made only for experimental purposes because, as mentioned, there is no logical way of determining the interrelationship of the seven variables.

THE SAMPLE

The sample includes the following 51 ccountries for which the data required for the calculation of the indicators were available by the end of 1982, about six months before the Mexican Payment difficulties came to public attention:

Australia	Honduras	Pakistan
Austria	Iceland	Paraguay
Belgium	Indonesia	Philippines
Bolivia	Ireland	South Africa
Brazil	Israel	Spain
Canada	Italy	Sri Lanka
Chile	Jamaica	Sweden
Colombia	Japan	Switzerland
Costa Rica	Kenya	Syria
Cyprus	Korea (South)	Tanzania
Ecuador	Malaysia	Thailand
Egypt	Malta	Tunisia
Finland	Mexico	Turkey
France	Morocco	United Kingdom
Germany	Netherlands	United States
Greece	New Zealand	Venezuela
Guatemala	Norway	Zambia

Malta and Sri Lanka are not listed in the March 1982 Institutional Investor Country Credit Ratings and are therefore not included in the comparative tables that follow. Tanzania and Zambia had a decline in their GER during some of the base periods: As a result the denominators of one of the variables becomes zero and, therefore, an indicator cannot be calculated.

COMPARISON OF FACTUAL REPAYMENT RISK INDICATORS WITH INSTITUTIONAL INVESTOR CREDIT RATINGS

The real test of the validity of a country evaluation system is its ability to anticipate future conditions, and since Institutional Investor Ratings reflect the prevalent opinion of the international bank community (see Chapter 8, under "Ratings Based on Evaluations of Leading International Banks"), it is important to determine whether the differences in placing between repayment risk indicators and Institutional Investor Ratings of the 47 countries in the sample has narrowed over time.

Table 23 reports "Factual External Repayment Risk Indicators" for the 47 countries in the sample, listed in increasing risk order. The range of each risk indicator, based on data of the periods 1978/80, 1979/80, and 1980, is reported in column 1; the other columns indicate the difference in place between end of 1981 repayment indicators and Instituional Investor ratings of March 1982 (column 2), March 1983 (column 3), and September 1983 (column 4). End of 1981 risk indicators, for instance, rank Mexico in 44th place, while the March 1982 Instituitional Investor ratings ranks it 2lst, with a difference of 23 places (column 2): March and September 1983 Institutional Investor ratings ranked Mexico 32nd with a difference of 12 places (columns 3 & 4).

The reader will, of course, keep in mind that the factual repayment risk indicator does not take into consideration social and political factors which weigh heavily in the evaluation of some country risks, such as Cyprus, Israel, South Africa, and Syria, or Guatemala and Honduras in troubled Central America.

Table 23   Factual External Repayment Risk Indicator—Low and High of 1978/1980, 1979/1980 and 1980.*

	Repayment Risk Indicator	Difference in Place Ranking with Institutional Investor Ratings		
		March 1982	March 1983	Sept. 1983
Switzerland	Cred. 85/Cred. 56	1	1	1
United States	Cred. 18/Cred. 3	1	1	1
France	Cred. 1/10	7	8	8
Germany	13/28	0	0	0
United Kingdom	15/29	2	0	0
Netherlands	32/34	3	2	2
Belgium	28/37	6	8	7
Japan	17/41	5	5	5
Italy	26/54	8	8	6
Austria	62/73	1	0	0
Cyprus	79/87	27	23	20
Ireland	63/88	6	7	7
Spain	54/89	6	5	5
Sweden	73/95	2	2	2
Norway	75/99	7	6	8
Finland	87/104	1	3	3
Malaysia	89/105	1	1	0
Israel	95/110	17	19	18
Canada	102/117	14	12	13
Australia	104/120	14	14	11

(continued)

Table 23 (*Continued*)

	Repayment Risk Indicator	Difference in Place Ranking with Institutional Investor Ratings		
		March 1982	*March 1983*	*Sept. 1983*
So. Africa	85/121	1	1	1
New Zealand	106/122	8	8	6
Egypt	85/123	14	12	10
Guatemala	72/130	19	20	20
Colombia	101/132	2	1	1
Thailand	122/137	3	1	3
Greece	97/145	4	4	5
Tunisia	126/150	4	1	1
Pakistan	123/152	12	12	12
Iceland	131/153	4	4	5
So. Korea	130/173	7	9	10
Syria	124/176	8	10	10
Philippines	161/176	1	0	2
Paraguay	146/177	1	3	5
Indonesia	179/207	10	10	11
Jamaica	185/217	10	7	7
Honduras	185/219	7	9	9
Turkey	207/230	7	2	2
Kenya	140/233	3	0	0
Morocco	194/234	1	2	3
Venezuela	179/240	21	20	13
Chile	247/270	14	12	8
Ecuador	251/293	12	7	5
Mexico	275/317	23	12	12
Bolivia	268/362	2	2	2
Brazil	321/383	16	18	16
Costa Rica	287/414	5	2	2

*Weight of components:

50%—GER increase indicator reciprocal.
      Current account imbalance as percentage of GER.
      Current account imbalance as percentage of GER increase.

100%—GER instability indicator.
      GER concentration indicator.
      Imbalance of external interest as percentage of GER.
      Imbalance of external interest plus imbalance of equity earnings as percentage of GER.

Source: Tables 12, 13, 16, 9, 10, 18, and 19.

Most readers will be surprised to see Japan in 8th place and will be even more surprised to find out that the reasons are poor export performance in 1979 (a 7 percent increase against a median of 23 percent for the sample, in SDR terms) and deficits in current account in 1979 and 1980.

Whether Japan is listed ahead or after Germany is academic; they are prime risks but are not going to pay more than 100 percent of what is due to creditors; one may add that France's repayment risk indicator is based on data of the 1978/1980 period, before Mitterrand came to power.

Canada did not place well because its "Imbalance of External Interest as Percentage of GER" was more than twice the median of the sample and its "Imbalance of External Interest Plus Imbalance of External Equity Earnings as percentage of GER" was one and one half times the median.

Australia, on the other hand, had a burden of "Imbalance External Interest Plus Imbalance of External Equity Earnings as Percentage of GER," almost twice the median, and "Current Account Deficit as Percentage of GER" and "Current Account Deficit as Percentage of GER Increase" between one and one half and two times the median of the sample.

At any rate the external repayment risk indicator should not be taken in isolation, it is only one part of the overall picture. For instance, some countries with very low per capita income may be unable to borrow abroad any significant amounts of money and may, as a result, have favorable external financial burden indicators (imbalance of external interest as percentage of GER) which will in turn tend to give them favorable external repayment risk indicators. Bangladesh is a good example: for the year 1980 it shows an excess of 5 million SDRs of interest earned abroad over interest paid. That, of course, does not make Bangladesh automatically a good credit risk. It may, however, indicate that there is room for some business.

One way of neutralizing such distortions is to classify countries on the basis of their access to private commercial and financial credit, following the World Bank classification mentioned in Chapter 10; namely:

I.   Countries that have not received IBRD loans or IDA credits during the preceding five years.
II.   Countries that have received IBRD loans but not IDA credits during the preceding five years.
III.   Countries that have received both IBRD loans and IDA credits during the preceding five years.

Of the 47 countries listed in Table 23, Bolivia, Egypt, Honduras, Indonesia, Kenya, Pakistan, the Philippines, and Thailand are in group III and presumably have limited access to private financing, and may, for that reason, have relatively favorable external repayment risk indicators.

PREDICTIVE QUALITIES OF FACTUAL REPAYMENT RISK INDICATORS

The main usefulness of repayment risk indicators is that they point out countries with poor external repayment capability, that could lead to payment difficulties. But, what are the predictive qualities of such indicators?

That is shown by the following summary of place differences between end of 1981 repayment risk indicators and subsequent Institutional Investor Country Credit Ratings listed in columns 2, 3, and 4 of Table 23:

| | Differences in Place Rankings | | |
	March 1982	March 1983	Sept. 1983
Total 47 countries	348	314	298
Index	100	90	86
Upper half, 24 countries	171	166	154
Index	100	97	90
Bottom half, 23 countries	177	148	144
Index	100	84	81

Even more significant is the decline of differences in place of the ten countries at the bottom of the list:

	March 1982	March 1983	Sept. 1983
Bottom ten countries	104	77	63
Index	100	74	61

The bottom ten countries are: Costa Rica, Brazil, Bolivia, Mexico, Ecuador, Chile, Venezuela, Morocco, Kenya, and Turkey (from the bottom up).

The progressive reduction in placing differences between end of 1981 repayment risk indicators and successive Institutional Investor rankings clearly indicates that the international banking community is gradually adopting external repayment risk concepts for country evaluation purposes. Especially significant is the downgrading by banks of the ten countries at the bottom of the repayment risk table.

END OF 1980 REPAYMENT RISK INDICATORS

End of 1981 repayment risk indicators should have warned prudent lenders, about six months before the Mexican difficulties, of the poor external repayment capability of most large borrowers. That would have helped; but did the indicators give a longer notice, for instance, at the end of 1980 to warn conservative lenders to stay away from some of the big borrowers?

The answer is yes, as shown by the following summary comparing repayment risk indicators calculated with data available at the end of 1980 with subsequent Institutional Investor rankings:

| | Differences in Place Rankings | | |
	March 1982	March 1983	Sept. 1983
Total 47 countries	340	306	288
Index	100	90	85
Upper half, 24 countries	169	162	155
Index	100	96	92
Bottom half, 23 countries	171	144	133
Index	100	84	78
Bottom ten countries	94	73	58
Index	100	78	62

The differences between end of 1980 and end of 1981 repayment risk rankings and subsequent Institutional Investor rankings are minor. Nine of the 1981 bottom ten countries were already there at the end of 1980; Morocco was not among the bottom ten, it replaced Guatemala.

The overall consistency of repayment risk indicators should not come as a surprise since they reflect mostly basic underlying conditions.

FACTUAL REPAYMENT RISK INDICATOR CHART

Some readers may find it difficult to interpret a table listing multiple evaluations for about 50 countries. To overcome this problem the countries could be subdivided into World Bank classification groups (see above) and the range of their repayment risk indicators could be reported in chart form.

Chart 1 shows repayment risk indicator ranges of 18 countries that have received International Bank for Reconstruction and Development (IBRD) loans but did not receive International Development Association (IDA) credits during the period July 1976 to June 1981 (Group II). Private lenders should be particularly interested in the repayment capability of this group, which includes countries that are considered creditworthy by the World Bank and are not yet industrialized.

The length of the bars on the chart indicates the spread between the low and high risk evaluation of each country, thus indicating the degree of uncertainty of the evaluation. Costa Rica, for instance, with a low of 287 and a high of 414 has a spread of 127 points, equal to 31 percent of the higher evaluation, while Cyprus with a low of 79 and a high of 87 has a spread of only 8 points, equal to 9 percent.

Countries whose risks are being evaluated could be pointed out by arrows, as done in the following chart, to indicate their relative position in the group.

Four countries, for which "Comparable Factual Risk Indicators" are reported in the following pages, are pointed out on the chart.

Chart 1   Group II—Factual Repayment risk Indicator—Low and High of 1978/1980, 1979/1980 and 1980.

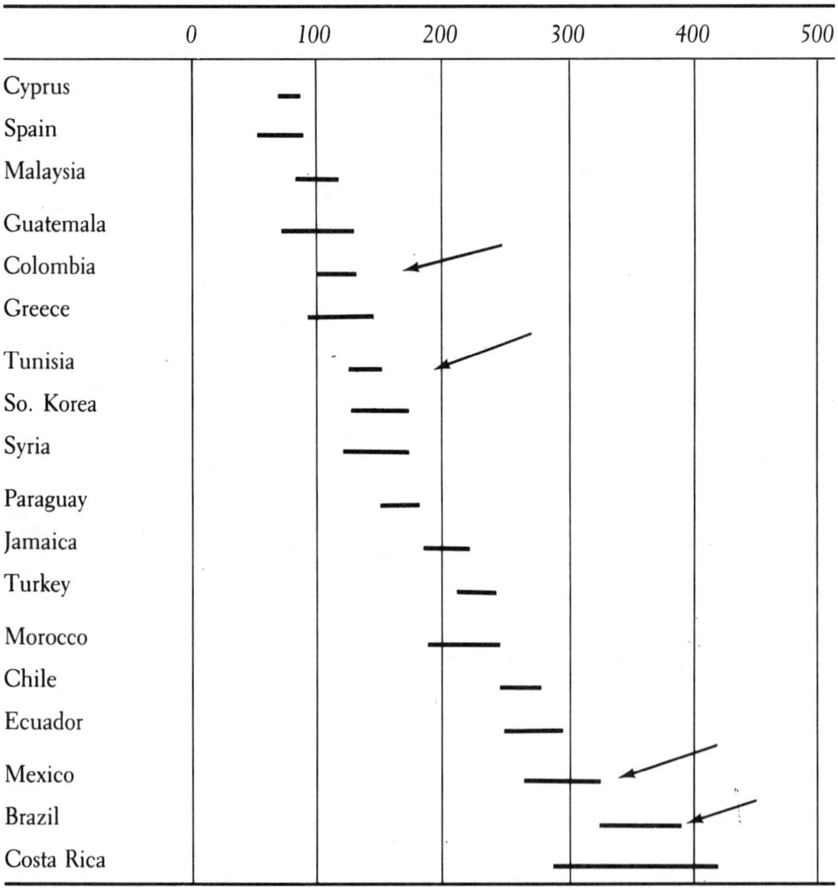

COMPARABLE FACTUAL COUNTRY RISK PROFILES

Four examples of comparable country risk profiles, prepared on the basis of data used in the experimental evaluations, are reported in the following pages to show how the factual part of a country report to be submitted to management may look.

The profiles report:

—   Factual Repayment Risk Indicator
—   Liquidity Risk Indicator
—   Per Capita Income Increase and Population Increase Risk Indicator
—   Purchasing Power Change Risk Indicator.

The comparison of Colombia and Tunisia, which have relatively low risk profiles, with Brazil and Mexico showing high risk profiles should be instructive.

Each profile indicates the World Bank group in which the country is placed and its share in global GER; the share in global GER should be compared with a country's share in a bank's overall international exposure.

Comparable Factual Risk Indicators

Colombia

January 1982		
World Bank Group II		0.27% of global GER
Factual Repayment Risk Indicator (1978/1980)		101–132
1. Relative GER generating capability		
–GER increases	122–149	
–GER instability indicator	71– 71	
–GER concentration indicator	302–348	
2. Overspending habits		
–Current account imbalance % GER	Cred. 54– 5	
–Current account imbalance % GER increase	Cred. 64– 4	
3. External financial burden		
–Imbalance external interest % GER	112–127	
–Imbalance external interest plus imbalance equity earnings % GER	73–100	
Liquidity Risk Indicator		75
1. External interest earned % interest due (1980)	89	

2.   Credit balances with banks % of amounts
     due to banks reporting to BIS–Sept. 1981   61

Per Capita Income Increase—Population Increase
Risk Indicator (averages 1978/1980)   121
     1.   Per capita income increase   71
     2.   Population increase   172
Purchasing Power Change Risk   112
     (Dollar adjusted CPI change % of dollar
     exchange rate adjustment)

Comments— Most indicators are favorable or within satisfactory limits, except GER concentration (coffee) which is three times the median, and population increase which is one of the ten highest in a sample of 51 countries.

Comparable Factual Risk Indicators

Tunisia

January 1982
World Bank Group II   1.17% of global GER

Factual Repayment Risk Indicator (1978/1980)   *126–150*
     1.   Relative GER generating capability
          –GER increase (reciprocal)   63–100
          –GER instability indicator   143–143
          –GER concentration indicator   175–199
     2.   Overspending habits
          –Current acccount imbalance % GER   83–135
          –Current account imbalance % GER
           increase   68– 89
     3.   External financial burden
          –Imbalance external interest % GER   137–153
          –Imbalance external interest plus imbalance
           equity earnings % GER   133–167
Liquidity Risk Indicator   99
     1.   External interest earned % interest due
          (1980)   78
     2.   Credit balances with banks % of amounts
          due to banks reporting to BIS–Sept. 1981 120

Per Capita Income Increase—Population Increase
Risk Indicator (averages 1978/80)   88
   1.   Per capita income increase   50
   2.   Population increase   127
Purchasing Power Change Risk   91
       (Dollar adjusted CPI change % of dollar
       exchange rate adjustment)

Comments— Most indicators are fair, however the External Financial Burden is on the high side and the GER Concentration Indicator is high (petroleum 27 percent, tourism 20 percent, and workers' remittances 9 percent in 1980).

Comparable Factual Risk Indicators

Brazil

      January 1982
      World Bank Group II   1.01% of global GER

Factual Repayment Risk Indicator (1978/1980)   321–383
     1.   Relative GER generating capability
          –GER increase   58–100
          –GER instability indicator   105–105
          –GER concentration indicator   36–44
     2.   Overspending habits
          –Current acccount imbalance % GER   490–542
          –Current account imbalance % GER
           increase   289–501
     3.   External financial burden
          –Imbalance external interest % GER   723–853
          –Imbalance external interest plus imbalance
           equity earnings % GER   485–532
Liquidity Risk Indicator   472
     1.   External interest earned % interest due
          (1980)   278
     2.   Credit balances with banks % of amounts
          due to banks reporting to BIS–Sept. 1981   667

Per Capita Income Increase—Population Increase

Risk Indicator (averages 1978/80)		117
1.	Per capita income increase	65
2.	Population increase	168
Purchasing Power Change Risk		86
	(Dollar adjusted CPI change % of dollar exchange rate adjustment).	

Comments— Most indicators are unfavorable, especially overspending and external financial burden, which are five to eight times median of countries in sample; liquidity indicators, 3 to 6 times worse than median. Good per capita income increase due in part to external borrowing. Good GER increase with low GER concentration.

Comparable Factual Risk Indicators

Mexico

January 1982
World Bank Group II   1.07% global GER

Factual Repayment Risk Indicator (1978/1980)			275–317
1.	Relative GER generating capability		
	–GER increase (reciprocal)	32– 47	
	–GER instability indicator	137–137	
	–GER concentration indicator	243–339	
2.	Overspending habits		
	–Current acccount imbalance % GER	267–308	
	–Current account imbalance % GER increase	109–159	
3.	External financial burden		
	–Imbalance external interest % GER	560–586	
	–Imbalance external interest plus imbalance equity earnings % GER	368–427	
Liquidity Risk Indicator			283
1.	External interest earned % interest due (1980)	333	
2.	Credit balances with banks % of amounts due to banks reporting to BIS–Sept. 1981	233	

Per Capita Income Increase—Population Increase
Risk Indicator (averages 1978/80)   118
   1.   Per capita income increase   38
   2.   Population increase   198
Purchasing Power Change Risk   137
        (Dollar adjusted CPI change % of dollar
        exchange rate adjustment).

Comments— Most indicators are unfavorable, especially external financial burden, which is 3 to 5 times median of countries in sample; liquidity is three times worse than median; population increase and purchasing power adjustment are among the five worst in sample. Good GER increase reflects petroleum exports, which went from 13 percent to 41 percent of GER during the three-year 1978/1980 period.

The comparable factual country risk profile is, of course, only the first step in the evaluation process. It has to be followed by the judgmental evaluation section; namely:

— judgmental economic factors,
— judgmental social and political factors, and
— conclusions.

The factual risk profile should be used as the foundation for the final evaluation. Executives should know where a country is placed by its factual external repayment capability; they should know to what extent a country's creditworthiness evaluation is based on factual comparable data, and to what extent on judgmental assessments of non-comparable factors.

CONCLUSIONS

The evaluation procedures suggested in this book are based on the premise that external debts may be repaid only with foreign exchange; they take into consideration present day conditions under which project lending by commercial banks is a rare exception, not the rule. Everyday private lending is a heterogeneous mixture of operations in which a country's economic development is only a remote consideration, the more so because a good share of the lending is to private enterprises. Creditworthiness evaluations of private lenders should focus on foreign exchange generating capability, not on domestic growth. Above all the evaluation should determine whether a country is over-burdened with external debts, which are, of course, the result of past over-spending.

Executives prefer one bottom line country evaluation, but they should be aware that there is no magic formula leading to an unequivocal overall country rating. The range of the multiple evaluations, suggested in this study for the overall country assessment, is an indication of the uncertainty of each evaluation and executives should know, and be reminded, of the uncertainty.

Country evaluation procedures are in a stage of accelerated evolution because many banks are dissatisfied with past results and are revising their systems. Moreover, new data useful for the evaluation are gradually becoming available and should be used in the assessment. Examples are the increase of the number of items reported for each country in the balance of payments statistics which went from 45 in the "Standard Presentation" used up to 1978, to 112 items in the subsequently introduced "Detailed Presentation." International Financial Statistics are also being expanded by the publication of various supplements, among them, starting with 1982, *Trade Statistics* which contains a "Trade by Commodity Section" indicating the share of "Manufactured Goods" in exports.

The suggestions outlined in this book should be, therefore, accepted on an interim basis, to be adapted to changing circumstances. Above all, analysts and executives should have an open mind about evaluation procedures and should be willing to explore any avenue that looks promising.

appendix 1

Balance of Payments Glossary*

Above the line (compare **below the line**).   Analysis of balance of payments accounts is accomplished most simply by choosing a significant point of cumulative balance, a point at which a line can be drawn to measure the country's surplus or deficit. From the point of view of a country's monetary authorities, international transactions above the line are those that must be financed; transactions below the line provide the financing. See also **autonomous transactions.**

Adjustment process.   The adjustment process in the balance of payments may be defined as the correction by the authorities of an imbalance, by inducing changes in the structure of the country's external transactions in order to eliminate economic distortions and pressures. It can be effected by general economic measures, such as realignment of the exchange rate or a change in the level of government expenditures, or by more specific measures, such as the regulation of imports or capital flows.

Aggregate presentation (see also **analytic presentation**).   The aggregate presentation largely reflects the analytic approach suggested in Chapter 7 of the Manual. The standard components of the balance of payments have been classified into seven standard groups that are considered relevant for analyzing the international economic relationship of the reporting countries in a uniform manner. The

*IMF Survey, February 5 and 19, 1979, pp. 40–42 and pp. 55–57; Balance of Payments Statistics, Volume 32, p. V.

groups that have been selected, however, do not necessarily reflect the Fund's recommendation about the analytic approach that would always be appropriate for countries to adopt for their own purposes. Moreover, the six balances that have been drawn in the presentation may be affected by special circumstances that must be taken into account when interpreting the figures that purport to measure any given concept of imbalance. Finally, the aggregate presentation must be read in the light of other developments in the national and world economic situation that also have a bearing on the surpluses and deficits that can be compiled from the standard components.

Analytic presentation (this presentation was used up to 1978—Volume 29 of the Balance of Payments Yearbook; in Volume 30 both Analytic and Aggregate Presentations are used; beginning with Volume 31 the **Aggregate Presentation** is used).   As distinguished from a standard presentation, an analytic presentation is a rearrangement of the original list of balance of payments items in order to give special emphasis to important groups of transactions. However, any presentation of a country's balance of payments is analytic to some extent. "Standard" should perhaps be interpreted to mean the presentation of the balance of payments that is customarily used; "analytic" should be interpreted to mean an alternative presentation designed to facilitate analysis for some particular purpose.

Assets.   This term commonly refers to financial assets that are claims on non-residents, from whose point of view the same item is a liability to a nonresident. Among reserve assets, however, gold and SDRs have a value which exists independently of any corresponding liabilities. Real assets such as merchandise, although they may be entered in company accounts as assets, are seldom described as assets in balance of payments analysis.

Autonomous transactions.   In the balance of payments, autonomous transactions are those undertaken for their own sake. Their net effect in each period is reflected in the net total of financing transactions. This analytic division of the balance of payments transactions into the two classes (autonomous and financing), though desirable, is difficult in practice. The same approach is described in different words under the terms **above the line** and **below the line.** In fact, the final group in a balance of payments table is rarely entitled "financing items," as this term would raise more questions than it would answer. A more readily identifiable term is usually possible—for example, "monetary movements" or "net reserves."

Balance of payments.   This is traditionally defined as the record of a country's international transactions with the rest of the world (or, in other words, transactions of its residents with nonresidents), together with a very few transactions, such as the monetization of gold, that do not fall under the main definition. The concept of the balance of payments may sometimes be broadened to include such movements as changes in the value of reserve assets resulting from fluctuations in value rather than from transactions themselves.

Basic balance.   Roughly defined as the balance of current and long-term capital transactions, the basic balance is intended to measure longer-term tendencies in the balance of payments and to show a balance that is not distorted by fluctuating, easily reversible, or speculative factors.

Below the line (compare **above the line**).   Transactions below the line are those in the balance of payments which, in some sense, provide the financing required to meet the country's surplus or deficit. At whatever point the line is drawn, the balance of transactions below the line must, by definition, match the balance above the line. See also **autonomous transactions.**

Capital account.   In the earliest published balance of payments statement, the capital account was given prominence as the term for the group of transactions that financed the current account. Although the financing function is now more often attributed to a much smaller group of transactions within the capital group (financing other capital, as well as current, account transactions), the capital account is of analytic interest in the Fund's presentations as it covers the net acquisition of financial assets.

Central monetary institutions.   This term represents the national authorities, such as the central bank or exchange office and the treasury of finance ministry, that mobilize finance to meet balance of payments deficits (or surpluses), for which purpose they have control over the national reserves. Alternatively, they may mobilize other means of financing to substitute for the use of reserves (see **exceptional financing**). Note that central monetary institutions' transactions cannot always be equated with reserve movements; the institutions may undertake long-term loan transactions or operate bilateral payments agreements that are not normally classed among reserves.

C.i.f. (cost, insurance, freight).   At the customs frontier of the importing country, the c.i.f. value of merchandise is recorded as including all international freight and insurance up to that point that must be paid by the importer. The c.i.f. valuation is seldom applied to exports. Note that "c.i.f. basis" is commonly used to denote that imports are recorded c.i.f., while exports are recorded f.o.b. Customs data on imports are published by the great majority of countries on a c.i.f. basis. Statistics on imports based on an exchange record are likely to be on a mixed basis, as actual payments recorded are sometimes c.i.f. and sometimes f.o.b.; this may also be true of exports in the exchange record. In the Fund's standard presentation (and detailed presentation) of the balance of payments, the f.o.b. basis is always used. See also **f.o.b.**

Contra-entries.   See **offsets.**

Counterpart items.   Certain items in the balance of payments exist only as counterpart items introduced to balance the inclusion of other items that do not fall naturally into the double-entry system. For example the monetization of gold by transfer from the nonmonetary sector to the monetary sector of the economy requires a counterpart entry, as the amount has been added to international reserves without an automatic offset in any other item of the international accounts. Similarly, the allocation of SDRs is another artificial counterpart item introduced into the balance of payments to offset the corresponding increase in SDR holdings.

Credits and debits. A credit in the balance of payments records the provision of goods or services, a decrease in holdings of a financial asset, or an increase in liabilities. Credits and debits form the two elements in the simple double-entry system used for recording the balance of payments. See also **double-entry system.**

Currency conversion rates. Under a regime of par values, a balance of payments expressed in terms of one currency can readily be converted into another currency by using the par values of the two currencies and disregarding the customary minor fluctuations that are permitted around those values in foreign exchange markets. At the other extreme, when currencies are floating, conversion factors must be obtained from market rates, and a large measure of approximation must be accepted, not only in conversions to a standard unit of account but also in the original compilation of a national balance of payments, since the balance of payments is an aggregate of transactions originally denominated in a variety of currencies. As a general rule, the shorter the period taken for conversion of flow data from one currency into another, at period averages, the more accurate the result will be. See also **market value.**

Current account. The current account comprises transactions in goods, services, and unrequited transfers, and it thus excludes transactions in financial assets and liabilities. This is the widest definition of the current account and the one generally accepted. At various times and in various countries there have been narrower definitions of the current account, and all or part of the category of unrequited transfers has been exluded; even investment income has sometimes been grouped with certain transfers and excluded from the current account. Some analysts prefer to exclude government transfers from the current account, while others exclude official aid grants: For this reason, whenever the terms current account is employed, it should be defined.

Deficit. A deficit in the balance of payments, usually reflected in a loss of reserves, implies that the economy's international receipts are exceeded by expenditures. Deficits can also be defined in other ways; deficits (or surpluses) on the trade balance, the current account balance, the basic balance, or the overall balance are all of interest in balance of payments analysis (see the definitions of those balances).

Detailed presentation. In this presentation, additional details may be shown for some of the 112 standard components, and those components for which the figures are zero or not available may be combined. The primary subdivision of the capital account is by function—direct investment, portfolio investment, other non-reserve capital, and reserves. Only within other non-reserve capital is there a subdivision by domestic sector—resident official sector, deposit money banks, and other sectors. Throughout "Capital, excluding reserves" there is a subdivision between long term and short term and between assets and liabilities. Drawings and repayments on loans are specified within the categories where they are likely to occur, as are liabilities constituting foreign authorities' reserves. Within "reserves," the principal subdivision is between the total change in holdings and the counterpart to valuation changes. Taken together, these two components equal the amount of reserve movements, adjusted to remove the effect of valuation changes.

Direct investment.   Although, in a general sense, direct investment is undertaken to acquire or prolong an interest in an enterprise, it has proved difficult to find an objective definition of it to use in balance of payments classification. Since the category has a dominant importance for most countries, compilers have used various rule-of-thumb definitions to identify direct investment transactions. Examples of transactions that can certainly be classified as direct investments are the setting up of branches or subsidiaries abroad, the purchase of shares that give a controlling voice in an enterprise, or the financing of extensions to plant and equipment in existing direct investments.

Double-entry system.   Because the accounting convention for recording the balance of payments requires two entries for each transaction, it is called a double-entry system. To take a simple example, one entry refers to what is bought and the other refers to what is paid for it. See also **credits and debits.**

Economic basis.   See **transaction basis.**

Entry.   This word is used in the normal accounting sense to mean the recording of a transaction or group of transactions in a specific item of the balance of payments accounts.

Errors and omissions.   The net total of errors and omissions is a balancing item that compensates for any excess of recorded credits over recorded debits (or vice versa). The total can be large when balance of payments statistics come from diverse sources, and can be of importance in analysis by suggesting, for example, a capital outflow (not otherwise recorded). A persistently large figure for net errors and omissions may lead to improvements in the statistics, if further inquiry reveals some major error such as a wrong valuation of merchandise. On the other hand, the absence of errors and omissions is more likely to suggest an unambitious balance of payments statement, based solely on self balancing banking statistics, rather than a comprehensive statement covering all appropriate categories, with all problems solved.

Exceptional financing.   Taken in conjunction with the use of (net) reserves, exceptional financing provides a measure of a country's balance of payments deficit (or surplus). The "exceptional financing" as defined for use in certain publications of the Fund, represents financing (other than use of reserves) mobilized by the authorities. For example, an entity other than the country's treasury or central bank may be induced by the authorities to borrow abroad rather than at home. In this example, although the borrower requires finance, it does not have to come from abroad, but the foreign currency obtained helps the authorities by providing general balance of payments support.

F.a.s. (free alongside ship). This is a variant of the f.o.b. convention for recording merchandise. Loading charges are excluded from the value recorded, which is otherwise the same as f.o.b.

Financing items. See **autonomous transactions.**

F.o.b. (free on board). This is the recommended method of recording merchandise for the balance of payments. Following the convention that exports and imports are valued at the custom frontier of the exporting country, all international freight and insurance beyond that point is excluded from the value of merchandise and included as "shipment" in the balance of payments. See also **c.i.f.**

Freight. On the f.o.b. basis of accounting (see **f.o.b.**), international freight is recorded entirely separately from the merchandise on which it is paid. For a given country, freight credits on the f.o.b. basis represent earnings on exports and on trade between other countries by carriers resident in that country; freight debits mainly represent payments on imports. See also **shipments.**

Gold. Two distinct roles in the balance of payments are played by gold. In one role it is akin to merchandise and may be exported and imported just like any other commodity (nonmonetary gold). In the other role, it is held by a country's authorities to form part of its international reserves; monetary gold may cross international frontiers in settlement of international indebtedness, and in this role it should be excluded from the merchandise totals. Nonmonetary gold enters into the balance of payments not only in a commodity role, but in other instances by the fact of "monetization," when gold is sold by mining companies or other residents to the authorities. An entry is then required in the balance of payments to offset the increase in international reserves, although there has been no international transaction. The reverse process of "demonetization" must also be recorded. See also **counterpart items.**

Government transactions. These transactions are grouped together in various areas of the Fund's standard (or detailed) presentation of the balance of payments, although they are not always specifically designated as official. Thus, exports and imports of the official sector are seldom distinguished in the merchandise item, and government transactions in transportation and travel are similarly merged into the totals for those categories. However, other governmental services are shown separately both for the domestic government and for foreign governments. The unrequited transfers of domestic and foreign governments are treated similarly, and official transactions are also specified in subdividing the capital account. In addition to the transactions of the central government, the official sector may include transactions of the central monetary authorities and local governments. Any international reserves held by the domestic government, rather than by central monetary institutions, are classified as reserves. See also **official and private sector.**

Gross. This term is used in balance of payments terminology as the antithesis of "net." See **net entries; net loans; net reserves.**

Imbalance. Although by definition the total of credit entries is equal to the total of debit entries, trends in certain items of the balance of payments may reflect distortions and strains in the domestic social accounts corresponding to imbalance. Thus an imbalance in the balance of payments will be seen as a deficit (or surplus) above the line, offset by the net amount of the transactions below the line; see also **above the line.**

Insurance. Insurance is generally separated into merchandise insurance (part of the shipment item) and nonmerchandise insurance (a detail of the components for miscellaneous services).

Investment income. This category includes: interest on loans, securities and deposits; Fund charges or distribution of income; dividends on shares; and profits of enterprises. Undistributed earnings are included in investment income and (with opposite sign) in the item for direct investment, with the result that there is no net impact on the balance of payments as a whole. Certain countries that have been unable to collect or estimate figures for undistributed earnings omit them from their balance of payments.

Invisibles. This term covers services and unrequited transfers and is used to distinguish those categories from visibles (merchandise) in the current account.

Leads and lags. When international payments for goods, services, or financial assets is accelerated or delayed (i.e., has leads or lags), it seems often to escape recording, as do other forms of short-term capital, and may thus fall into the item "net errors and omisions" (see also **errors and omissions**).

Liabilities. In balance of payments terminology, liabilities are the financial claims of nonresidents. See also **assets.**

Long-term. This expression is used in the balance of payments to describe a security or other financial instrument with an original maturity of more than one year or with no stated maturity. An analysis of the capital account into short-term and long-term elements is perhaps less interesting than an analysis by sector or by function, but long-term characteristics can sometimes be a useful criterion for choosing the items that enter into the basic balance (see also **basic balance**).

Losses. When they result from unprofitable direct investment enterprises, losses are usually entered in the balance of payments as deductions from investment income. Thus negative entries (minus credits or minus debits) can occasionally result when the direct investment enterprises have had losses during a given period. Losses or gains in reserves resulting from changes in currency values are, under some definitions of the balance of payments, included with the losses resulting from transactions (see also **counterpart items**); in other statements, losses from changes in value are excluded from the balance of payments.

Market value. Merchandise should be valued at market price in the balance of payments, but it is more likely to have been recorded at the value given by the customs or at the price actually paid, either of which presumably give a reasonable approximation to market price. Market values should also be used, and are more readily available, for conversion from one currency or unit of account to another, on which many figures in the balance of payments are based. Average rates for the period concerned can be worked out from market quotations.

Merchandise. Almost all of the exports and imports by a given country are entered in the merchandise account of the balance of payments. The criterion for inclusion is an international change of ownership, and the timing of the inclusion should correspond to the time when ownership changes. The few types of goods that change ownership but are not covered by the merchandise account include travelers' purchases abroad (which form part of the travel component) and purchases of goods by diplomatic and military personnel (classified under other official goods, services, and income).

Migration. Effective transfers by migrants are recorded in the balance of payments when the individual moves his residence (or center of interest) from one national economy to another. His residence may be established under tax laws or exchange control regulations; in the absence of other criteria, a stay in the new country for one year or more makes it probable that the individual has migrated. See also **residence**.

Multilateral settlements. See **regional statements**.

Net. This term is used in the balance of payments as the antithesis of gross.

Net entries. In net entries, the debits have been set off against the credits. A net entry for travel measures the net effect of resident travelers' expenditures abroad and foreign travelers' expenditures in the reporting country.

Net loans. This is an ambiguous term, as offsetting may occur in either of two ways: loan drawings may be offset against repayments, or transactions in loans extended may be offset against loans received. The meaning of net loans should always be clearly defined in a parenthetical explanation or an explanatory footnote.

Net reserves. Gross reserves comprise assets only; net reserves refer to gross assets less liabilities constituting foreign authorities' reserves.

Nonmonetary capital. Although this term sounds contradictory, it is commonly used as a brief description of the category comprising the capital transactions of the nonmonetary sectors (nonbank sectors) of the economy.

Nonresidents. Since the balance of payments can be defined broadly as the transactions of a country's residents, with all nonresidents, it follows that nonresidents are "the rest of the world" with which these transactions take place.

Official sector. A useful distinction is maintained between "government sector" or "general government sector," on the one hand, covering the actual governmental institutions of the central, state, and local governments, and the "official sector", on the other hand, with a wider coverage that also includes central monetary institutions. Such institutions as, for example, the U.S. Federal Reserve System are not strictly part of the central government but may be linked to it for analytic purposes. See also **government transactions** and **private sector.**

Offsets. Every entry in the balance of payments has its off-setting entry, or entries, explicitly or implicitly in some other item that is of opposite sign. These are the "contraentries" of double-entry accounting (see **double-entry systems**). For example, a transaction in goods or services may be reflected in a movement in a foreign account in a commercial bank and thus give rise to a balance of payments offset in the monetary sector of the capital account; a gift in kind may be recorded under merchandise, with an offset under unrequited transfers.

Overall balance. This is the balance that must be financed by gross or net reserve movements. The overall balance comprises the basic balance and also the short-term, readily reversible transactions normally excluded from the basic balance. In Fund presentations the overall balance has often been shown in more than one way; for example, it may exclude the allocation of SDRs or it may include them. See also **autonomous transactions.**

Payments balance. This is a popular term used in approximately the same sense as overall balance. Its use indicates the presence of a dangerous, but understandable, wish to quote the single figure that will summarize the balance of payments surplus or deficit for the period. The balance of payments is best understood by considering various cumulative balances, such as trade balance, current account balance, basic balance, and overall balance.

Payment basis (or settlement basis). A balance of payments described as being on this basis is normally taken from an exchange record and is a first approximation to a more comprehensive statement (see **transaction basis**).

Payments imbalance. This usually means deficit but sometimes means surplus. See also **imbalance.**

Portfolio investment. As distinguished from direct investment (undertaken for the sake of obtaining entrepreneurial income), portfolio investment is undertaken for the sake of obtaining investment income or capital gains.

Private sector. For balance of payments analysis, the domestic economy is usually subdivided into the official and private sectors. The latter, which might also be described as the enterprise sector (and includes government-owned enterprises) is that part of the economy most likely to be affected by market forces; it may include deposit money banks. The distinction between official and private is seldom maintained throughout every category of transactions listed in balance of payments presentations. In Fund tables, the distinction is overridden in the case of many items where alternative analyses are preferred. See also **official sector.**

Regional statements. A regional balance of payments statement may be difficult to compile and to interpret when multilateral use of currency is permitted and the currency used for settlement need not be the currency of one of the transacting countries; a reconciliation item should be provided in a regional table, for each region specified, in the form of an entry against "multilateral settlements" (or, failing that, against net errors and omissions). Regional balance of payments statements continue to be of interest to analysis of regional groups such as the European Community and the free-trade areas in Latin America, but the Fund does not make recommendations about the rules for compiling such statements. A regional statement is of greatest interest where trade and payments are on strict bilateral lines, but in such situations balance of payments statistics are seldom available for publication.

Reserve creation. Reserves can be created by the allocation of SDRs, the monetization of gold, and the classification of financial assets as reserves, and they can be destroyed by the reversal of those processes. In addition, since reserves are expressed in terms of a currency or a unit of account, realignments of currencies can change the value of reserves expressed in terms other than those of the currency held.

Reserve gains. See **losses.**

Reserves. Reserves are the actual (spot) holdings of SDRs, gold and foreign exchange assets, together with Fund positions, available to the monetary authorities to meet balance of payments deficits. Certain categories are conventionally excluded from reserves, such as long-term loans and payments agreement balances because of their limited availability. Assets held in nominally long-term form are often included, however, if they are readily marketable.

Residence. This is an important criterion in deciding on the transactions to be included in the balance of payments, as most transactions recorded are between residents of different countries. An individual is regarded as resident of a reporting country if his principal center of interest is in that country. An individual in a country for less than one year might be regarded as a visitor rather than as a resident (see also **migration** and **travel**). Similar criteria determine the residence of an enterprise.

Services ("invisible services"). In the balance of payments, services are conventionally listed under the principal categories of shipment, other transportation, travel, investment income, other official services, and other private services (including insurance other than the merchandise insurance usually classified with transportation). Services are included, together with merchandise (including nonmonetary gold) and private and official unrequited transfers, in the current account in the widest of its definitions.

Settlement basis. See **payment basis.**

Shipment. This signifies international carriage of goods, comprising the services traditionally known as freight, insurance, and other distributive services on merchandise.

Short-term. This expression is used in the balance of payments to describe a security or other financial instrument having an original maturity of one year or less. See also **long-term.**

Special drawing rights (SDRs). Since the allocation of SDRs is an act of reserve creation, SDRs, like monetary gold, are assets that have no corresponding liability. In the balance of payments, the allocation of SDRs (credit) form the counterpart that matches the increase (debit) in a country's holdings of SDRs, which form part of reserves. At the national level, most central bank balance sheets include SDRs as assets, and they are offset on the liability side by an entry for allocations of SDRs.

Standard presentation (this presentation was used up to 1978—Volume 29 of the Balance of Payments Yearbook; in Volume 30 both Standard and Detailed Presentations are used; beginning with Volume 31 the **Detailed Presentation** is used). This is a listing of balance of payments components in a conventional order as standardized by the Fund.

Surplus. A surplus in the balance of payments is reflected in a gain in reserves, implying that the economy's international receipts exceed expenditures. See also **deficit** for other possible definitions.

Trade balance. Of the several cumulative balances that can be used in analyzing the balance of payments, the trade balance is usually the most important as it comprises merchandise, a category which often contains the largest amounts shown in the statement. Since merchandise figures are normally available soon after the end of each month, they provide an early indication of balance of payments trends, even though the figures may not have been fully adjusted to fit into a balance of payments framework. The trade balance based on unadjusted customs statistics includes amounts of freight and insurance where imports have been valued c.i.f.; it may include goods such as contractors' equipment entering the country without change of ownership; it may exclude the value of ships and aircraft entering service abroad and never recorded as imports. There are many other differences in coverage, timing and valuation between customs totals and the fully adjusted balance of payments totals. These differences are usually small but can on occasion be large, and the unadjusted trade balance must be used with caution as an indicator of developments.

Transaction basis. This term, synonymous with "economic basis," is sometimes used to denote a balance of payments appropriately compiled to cover the transactions that have taken place rather than to reflect the receipts and payments to which they give rise. A simple example of the difference in approach is found in the recording of debt that is due but not paid. Nothing is recorded on the "payment basis," but in the full statement on the transaction basis, repayment is recorded when due, financed by a new liability arising from nonpayment. Similarly, merchandise purchased on credit is recorded, on a payment basis, only when paid for; on a transaction basis, the purchaser's goods would be recorded when he obtained them, with an offsetting entry under trade credit. The later settlement of the trade credit would give rise to further entries in the balance of payments.

Transaction value. In valuing merchandise, where no readily ascertainable transaction value exists, the compiler will often have to use a transaction value represented perhaps by the value quoted in the market. See also **market value.**

Transfer payments, transfers, unilateral transfers. These are all terms that have been used in the past in the sense of unrequited transfers, an expression used in later volumes of the IMF Balance of Payments Yearbook and in the fourth edition of the Balance of Payments Manual. It has been adopted as the Fund's standard description since it is self explanatory. See also **unrequited transfers.**

Transportation (see also **shipment**). In addition to freight on international shipments, transportation in the balance of payments includes, for example, the following categories of services: passenger fares, time-chartering of ships and aircraft, port disbursements (including bunkering, ship stores, and repairs), airport disbursements, mail fees, salvage earnings, and earnings from foreign coastal trade.

Travel. In the balance of payments, travel covers visitors' expenditures within the country they are visiting, but it does not cover their transportation expenses to or from that country. The category covers living expenses, entertainment, purchases of goods and transportation within the country visited. Visitors include tourists, businessmen, government officials, students, pilgrims, and invalids seeking treatment. A visitor staying longer than one year is considered to be a resident of the country.

Undistributed earnings. The earnings of an enterprise, not distributed to the direct investors but reinvested in the enterprise, are included in the balance of payments statements. Thus these earnings (offset by new investment) are recorded on the one side, and the full amount of new investment by nonresidents is recorded on the other side. See also **investment income.**

Unit of account.   A balance of payments statement is ideally expressed in terms of a stable unit of account. A series of figures expressed in a currency that has been frequently revalued is meaningless for international comparisons and sometimes even for domestic consideration. Until 1971, the U.S. dollar was the currency of account most often used for balance of payments statements. In Fund publications, the SDR is now normally used as the unit of account.

Unrequited transfers.   Broadly, unrequited transfers are transactions undertaken without a quid pro quo and were previously known as transfer payments (see above), unilateral transfers, or donations. The term "unrequited transfers" has been taken from national income accounting (although balance of payments accounts seldom follow the national income accounts in subdividing these transfers into current and capital). In the balance of payments, unrequited transfers are conventionally included in the current account, although a part of government transfers may in some analyses be included with certain loans to make a total for official aid.

Valuation.   A correct valuation basis for merchandise, securities, or currencies is often a problem for the balance of payments compiler, who should aim to record the value used in each transaction. Approximations must often be accepted. See also **market value** and **transaction value.**

Visible trade.   This refers to merchandise trade (see **merchandise**) as distinct from "invisible trade" in services, income, or unrequited transfers.

Workers' earnings (see also **migration** and **residence**).   Wages and salaries earned by workers visiting the reporting country should be recorded in full as debits in the services components of the balance of payments as earnings by nonresidents, and the temporary workers' expenditures should be recorded as credits in the same components (the balance being assumed to have been remitted to the workers' home country). If the worker remains for more than one year, he is regarded as a resident and his earnings and expenditures are no longer recorded in the balance of payments. In practice, many countries are able to record only the net remittance, and there may be various criteria for residence; thus, the statistics for workers' earnings may not be comparable from country to country.

Index